Blue Heaven

Los Angeles Dodgers
World Series Champions

A Story 32 Years in the Making

Book design by **ANDREA ZAGATA** and **JOSH CRUTCHMER**

Cover photo credits
Top left: Kyodo via AP Images | Top right: Photo by Tom Pennington/Getty Images
Bottom: AP Photo/Tony Gutierrez

ISBN: 978-1-940056-89-0

Printed in the United States of America

Unforgettable!

Los Angeles Dodgers – World Champions!

Sounds pretty good doesn't it? Dodger fans have waited 32 long years to utter those words, and finally, the Boys in Blue are back on top.

Let the celebration begin!

In what has to be considered one of the craziest Major League seasons on record, the Dodgers showed their dominance from the get go. A delayed start to the season and no fans in the stands had no effect on this Dodgers squad as they jumped out to a 22-8 record in the first month of action and never looked back. A seven-game winning streak in mid-August helped propel the Dodgers to become the first team to lock in a spot in the expanded playoffs. After making quick work of Milwaukee in the Wild-Card round and San Diego in the Divisional Series, the Dodgers locked horns with the Atlanta Braves in one of the all-time great National League Championship Series. Trailing 3 games to 1 the Dodgers stormed back winning Games 5 and 6 to set up a winner take all Game 7. A generation of Dodgers fans will remember where they were when Cody Bellinger blasted a 400-ft home run to give LA a 4-3 lead late in Game 7 and then watched as Julio Urias completed the miraculous comeback with three shutout innings to clinch the pennant. As if that wasn't enough excitement the Dodgers took things up another notch with big hit after big hit in their World Series win over a scrappy Tamp Bay Rays team.

In the following pages we proudly bring you on a trip down memory lane of this championship season that came to its jubilant conclusion in Arlington, Texas.

Blue Heaven provides Dodgers fans the best view in the house of all the ups and downs of the season and gives you an inside look at the incredible World Series win 32 years in the making.

Our heartfelt congratulations go out to President of Baseball Operations Andrew Friedman, Manager Dave Roberts and his staff, and the entire Dodgers team on their accomplishments this season.

Celebrate this season LA, and save this book to revisit the Dodgers' magical moments and unforgettable team – both stars and role players – who rewarded your faith with a World Championship.

Congratulations Los Angeles Dodgers! Let's do it again soon.

The Los Angeles Dodgers take batting practice before Game 1 of the World Series.
AP PHOTO/TONY GUTIERREZ

Fan-less Opener

Dodgers beat Giants 8-1 behind Hernandez' 5 RBI

July 23, 2020

Los Angeles — Mookie Betts singled in the seventh inning for his first hit as a Los Angeles Dodger, then signaled for the ball.

That, along with the lineup card, is headed for a display in his house.

"This is something I'll always remember," he said Thursday night after scoring the go-ahead run in an 8-1 opening victory over the San Francisco Giants in a fan-less stadium. "It's just a new chapter in life."

Betts went 1 for 5 with two strikeouts, a day after signing a $365 million contract covering 2021-32.

Betts spoke without his bat when he kneeled during the national anthem. Teammates Cody Bellinger and Max Muncy stood resting a hand on each of his shoulders. Giants manager Gabe Kapler, in his first game as Bruce Bochy's successor, kneeled, too.

"It was just unity," Betts said. "We're all on the same team, we're all here for change, even the Giants."

Betts' perspective on kneeling has changed since 2016, when he said he wouldn't take such action. His father, Willie, served in Vietnam with the U.S. Air Force.

"I wasn't educated, and that's my fault," Betts said. "I know my dad served and I'll never disrespect the flag, but there also has to be change. Kneeling is for the injustice."

Kike Hernandez homered and drove in five runs while tying his career high with four hits for Los Angeles.

"It's a great feeling," he said.

Justin Turner grounded into a fielder's choice and Betts beat second baseman Donovan Solano's throw to the plate to give the Dodgers a 2-1 lead in the seventh. The Giants lost their video challenge of the call after Betts slid head-first.

"If that out is recorded at the plate, I think we're talking about a much different game," Kapler said.

Betts struck out with the bases loaded, ending a five-run inning that made it 6-1.

Adam Kolarek (1-0) got the victory with 1 2/3 innings of relief.

Dustin May became the first Dodgers rookie to start on opening day since Fernando Valenzuela in 1981 after Clayton Kershaw went on the injured list because of a back issue. It was similar to when Valenzuela was a late replacement for the injured Jerry Reuss back then.

"He kept his composure," Hernandez said. "He wasn't nervous or intimidated by the amount of cardboards we had in the stands."

May allowed one run and seven hits in 4 1/3 innings. The 6-foot-6 right-hander struck out four and walked none.

"It's the kind of thing you dream about, throwing on opening day," May said. "Once the first pitch was thrown I was all good and ready to get going."

May originally was not on the 30-man active roster, and the 22-year-old found himself pressed into duty after Kershaw's back stiffened during a weight room workout on Tuesday.

Pablo Sandoval's sacrifice fly scored San Francisco's lone run. Tyler Rogers (0-1) took the loss.

The sounds of the game were amplified with only cardboard cutouts of fans in areas of the stands. The crack of the bat on a sharply hit ball. The DJ's music echoing. Foul balls clunking loudly upon landing in the seats. The home plate umpire's third-strike calls easily heard. Teammates yelled reminders to Dodgers left fielder Joc Pederson about which base to throw to after he snagged a fly ball in the second.

At right: Cody Bellinger, left, and Max Muncy put their hands on Mookie Betts' shoulder in a show of solidarity during the national anthem on Opening Day.

Facing: Kike Hernandez is congratulated by Justin Turner after hitting a solo home run during the eighth inning.

AP PHOTOS/ MARK J. TERRILL

Mookie Betts beats the tag by Giants catcher Tyler Heineman during seventh inning action.
AP PHOTO/MARK J. TERRILL

Message Sent

Benches clear
as Dodgers
beat Astros
5-2

July 28, 2020

HOUSTON — The Houston Astros are trying to put their sign-stealing scandal behind them.

It seems as if the Los Angeles Dodgers have their own thoughts on the matter.

Benches cleared during the Dodgers' 5-2 victory over the Astros in the first game between the teams since it was revealed that Houston stole signs en route to a 2017 World Series championship that came at Los Angeles' expense.

The fracas occurred after Dodgers reliever Joe Kelly threw high-and-tight pitches to Astros stars Alex Bregman and Carlos Correa in the sixth inning.

"Balls get away sometimes but not that many in the big leagues," Houston manager Dusty Baker said. "When you throw a 3-0 fastball over a guy's head you're flirting with ending his career."

The Dodgers had a 5-2 lead after a five-run fifth when Kelly, who was with Boston in 2017 and also faced Houston that postseason, threw behind Bregman for ball four. Bregman grimaced after jumping to avoid being hit, then trotted to first base.

There were two outs in the inning when Kelly threw an errant breaking ball over Correa's head. Correa, who homered and finished with three hits, took off his batting helmet and stared Kelly down before continuing the at-bat.

Kelly struck out Correa, then stuck out his tongue and made a face in his direction. Correa started walking toward him and the players exchanged words, prompting the benches to clear in the first such incident of this pandemic-delayed season. There was plenty of yelling and crowding -- outlawed as MLB tries to play a 60-game season amid the pandemic -- but there was no pushing or punches thrown.

Baker said things really got out of hand because of something he said Kelly told Correa after the strikeout.

"What really enraged everybody ... is when he told him: `Nice swing (expletive)," Baker said. "What are you supposed to do then?"

Baker was asked if the Astros said anything to provoke Kelly.

"We didn't say anything," he said. "We don't start nothing. But we don't take nothing either."

Kelly denied that he purposely threw at the Astros. He was asked if there was any added motivation Tuesday since his Red Sox team lost to Houston in the AL Division Series in 2017.

"No. When I was with the Red Sox we beat them in '18," he said. "It's one of those things that I pitch competitively. With no fans here, it's easy to hear some stuff (from the opposing dugout) ... there's something they apparently didn't take too kind to."

Dodgers manager Dave Roberts wasn't sure if Kelly's errant throws were retaliation for Houston's cheating.

"I really don't know, to be quite honest," he said. "I know he got behind Bregman 3-0 and lost a fastball. I really don't think there was intent behind that. I think those guys took a little bit of offense. Even the one to Correa, that was a breaking ball that just backed up."

"Obviously the expectation going into the series that things were kind of escalated maybe a little, I don't know if prematurely is the word, but that's kind of what happened."

Order was restored after a couple of minutes and there were no ejections, but Baker was still upset before play resumed and got in the face of an umpire.

Bregman avoided questions about the incident postgame and Correa did not speak to reporters.

Houston was punished by the commissioners' office in January for the sign-stealing scheme, which led to the firing of general manager Jeff Luhnow and manager AJ Hinch. But many players around the league were unhappy that no players were disciplined for their roles in the cheating.

The Dodgers had harsh words for the Astros during spring training, but Roberts said before the game that he didn't think his team would retaliate.

Brusdar Graterol (1-1) struck out two in a scoreless fifth for the win. Kenley Jansen allowed one hit in a scoreless ninth for the save.

Facing: Benches clear after Astros shortstop Carlos Correa strikes out in the bottom of the sixth inning.
LESLIE PLAZA JOHNSON/
ICON SPORTSWIRE

Joe Kelly yells back at Carlos Correa.
AP PHOTO/DAVID J. PHILLIP

Mookie Mania!

Betts ties
MLB mark
with 3 of
Dodgers'
6 HRs

August 13, 2020

LOS ANGELES — Mookie Betts hit three home runs Thursday night -- for the sixth time in his career.

Now nobody's done it more often.

Betts launched half of the season-high six long balls socked by the Los Angeles Dodgers during an 11-2 rout of the San Diego Padres. His sixth three-homer game matched the major league mark shared by Sammy Sosa and Hall of Famer Johnny Mize.

Betts accomplished the feat in 813 career games. Sosa needed 2,364, and Mize did it in 1,884.

"I just think it's pretty cool, but it's not as important as the rings," Betts said.

The four-time All-Star went 4 for 4 with five RBI and was hit by a pitch in the leadoff spot, where manager Dave Roberts has been reluctant to lock him in.

However, with Corey Seager back in the lineup after injury, Roberts turned to Betts at the top.

"I've been doing it my whole life so I think I'm just comfortable there," Betts said. "It's just one of those things where you only lead off once, but I enjoy getting things started and creating havoc on the basepaths."

Betts signed one of the richest contracts in baseball history last month, agreeing to a $365 million, 12-year deal on the eve of opening day, and has mostly batted second in this pandemic-shortened season. The 2018 AL MVP said when he was acquired from Boston in a blockbuster trade last offseason that he thought he'd be hitting leadoff with his new team.

"I'm definitely here to do whatever is best for the team," said Betts, who talked to Roberts again recently about the leadoff spot. "I think he's just trying to find a comfort in the lineup in general."

Roberts knew the kind of special player the Dodgers landed in Betts, although the 5-foot-9 right fielder has surprised him in one way.

"I know he hits homers," the manager said, "but it's more power than I expected."

With a chance to tie the big-league record of four home runs in one game, Betts reached on an infield single in the seventh.

When Betts wasn't chasing down balls in the outfield or rocketing them into the empty stands, he was on the bench talking hitting with his teammates.

"He's just very unselfish," Roberts said.

The National League's top two home run-hitting teams split the four-game series, with the Dodgers outscoring the Padres 17-2 over the last two.

"We wanted to win this series," San Diego starter Chris Paddack said. "I just felt I can do a better job of, I keep saying it, but one of those things is to eliminate the damage. But it just kept going and going and going. Overall tough, tough loss."

Julio Urias (2-0) gave up consecutive two-out solo homers to Tommy Pham and Eric Hosmer in the first after the Padres failed to homer for the first time in nine games during a 6-0 loss Wednesday night.

The Dodgers answered right back in the bottom of the inning to tie it 2-all. Betts was hit by a pitch and scored on Seager's two-run shot to right on an 0-2 pitch from Paddack (2-2). Seager returned after missing five games because of lower back discomfort. AJ Pollock added a go-ahead solo homer with two outs.

Los Angeles scored in each of the first five innings. Betts connected on a two-run shot to left field with two outs in the second for a 5-2 lead.

Pollock's RBI double made it 6-2 in the third.

Austin Barnes and Betts went deep back-to-back in the fourth, extending the Dodgers' lead to 9-2. Barnes' two-run shot landed in the left-field pavilion and Betts followed with a solo shot to the same area.

Betts wasn't finished. He smashed a two-run homer in the fifth for an 11-2 lead.

"He's impressive," Seager said.

The Dodgers' offensive outburst didn't include reigning NL MVP Cody Bellinger, who went 0 for 3 with a strikeout and a walk before being replaced.

Urias allowed two runs and five hits in 6 1/3 innings. He struck out three and walked none.

Paddack gave up six runs and six hits in three innings. He struck out one and walked one.

Mookie Betts celebrates after hitting a solo home run in the fourth inning – one of three home runs on the day for the star outfielder.
AP PHOTO/
KIRBY LEE

Mookie Betts hits his third home run of the game against San Diego.
KIYOSHI MIO/ICON SPORTSWIRE VIA AP

Powerball!

Dodgers
pound
7 homers
to get sweep
of Rockies

August 23, 2020

LOS ANGELES — Kike Hernandez hit a three-run drive, crossed the plate and motioned taking a 3-point jumper in a tribute to Kobe Bryant on what would have been the late NBA superstar's 42nd birthday.

"It's probably one of those that I'll always remember," Hernandez said. "We lost Kobe a little too soon."

Mookie Betts went deep twice in the Dodgers' seven-homer attack, powering Los Angeles past the Colorado Rockies 11-3 for a three-game sweep.

"We like when it's warm in here," Hernandez said, referring to the game-time temperature of 91 degrees. "When it's a little cooler the ball tends to die. The last four games at home has been pretty warm and we've enjoyed that."

The Dodgers are the only team in the majors yet to lose a series, unbeaten in 11. They have won 11 of 12 games overall and own the best record in baseball at 22-8 at the halfway point of this abbreviated season.

"The simple truth of this series is they outpitched us and they outhit us," Rockies manager Bud Black said. "They came in with a lot of momentum, they were playing well, and they continued."

Wearing sunglasses at the plate, Hernandez's three-run shot with two outs in the fourth inning lifted the Dodgers to a 5-2 lead. Joc Pederson singled and Max Muncy reached on an infield single to set up the Dodgers' third homer of the game.

Cody Bellinger, the reigning NL MVP, hit a leadoff drive in the sixth and Will Smith led off the seventh with a homer, extending the Dodgers' lead to 7-2. Muncy went deep leading off the eighth. Betts added a two-run shot to right with two outs for his 11th homer.

The last time the Dodgers belted seven homers was Sept. 2 at home against the Rockies.

Victor Gonzalez (1-0) earned his first major league victory, allowing one hit and striking out two in two innings of relief.

Pinch hitter AJ Pollock hit a bases-loaded sacrifice fly for Los Angeles in the seventh for the game's only run that didn't score via homer.

The Dodgers took the lead on Corey Seager's solo shot in the first. The Rockies tied it on Trevor Story's two-out homer in the third.

Betts put the Dodgers ahead 2-1 with a two-out blast to center in the third. The Rockies tied it again on Ryan McMahon's homer leading off the fourth on Ross Stripling's first pitch of the inning.

The only Dodger without a hit was Chris Taylor. He walked twice.

Sam Hilliard hit a solo homer in the ninth for Colorado.

Antonio Senzatela (3-1) gave up the first four Dodgers homers after allowing just four in his first 31 innings of the season. The right-hander allowed six runs and seven hits in 5 1/3 innings.

The Rockies continued to sputter. They have lost a season-high seven straight in the midst of playing 20 consecutive games. Colorado has dropped 10 of 11 overall after starting the season with an 11-3 mark.

"We still have the confidence and the hope we'll get this thing back on the right track," Story said. "Honestly, I don't think it takes a lot, one or two games to get us on a roll and get that monkey off our back."

Corey Seager rounds
the bases after hitting
a solo home run
against Colorado.
AP PHOTO/
ALEX GALLARDO

Enrique Hernandez celebrates with Joc Pederson after hitting a three-run home run as Rockies catcher Elias Diaz looks away.
AP PHOTO/ALEX GALLARDO

Bay Area Beatdown

Kershaw wins third straight, Dodgers beat Giants

August 27, 2020

SAN FRANCISCO — Clayton Kershaw struck out four and didn't walk a batter over six scoreless innings Thursday, leading the Los Angeles Dodgers past the San Francisco Giants 7-0 a day after he spoke out in support of his Black teammates as the clubs decided not to play in protest of racial injustice.

"For guys to stand together and not play a major league baseball game is a big deal," Dodgers manager Dave Roberts said before Thursday's first game of two seven-inning contests in a doubleheader.

AJ Pollock hit a two-run homer and Dodgers star Mookie Betts reached 1,000 hits in his 824th game with his sixth-inning single. The souvenir ball was quickly retrieved, authenticated and put in a protective box.

And Betts nearly didn't play again.

He initially planned to sit out Thursday after speaking to Roberts late Wednesday, then changed his stance.

Roberts said the Dodgers stayed together in deciding how to proceed Thursday.

"Regardless of the doubleheader he wasn't going to play, felt that he wanted to continue to stand firm on his position, which I absolutely respect and support" Roberts said. "But in talking to him this morning ... talking to the Players Alliance and Black players around the league, they just came to the consensus that they could use their platform more by playing today, playing both games. And also the fact that there's a lot of white teammates that stood beside them in not playing, acknowledging that and to continue to stay unified and play and to stay in lockstep with their teammates was very important."

Kershaw (4-1) won his third straight start and avenge a loss to the Giants on Aug. 8. Josh Sborz completed the four-hit shutout.

Kershaw's delivery a night earlier was equally impressive.

"As a white player on this team is how do we show support? What's something tangible that we can do to help our black brothers on this team?" Kershaw said in support of Betts not playing Wednesday. "Once Mookie said that he wasn't going to play that really started our conversation as a team of what we could do to support that."

He said he went to bed Wednesday expecting Los Angeles to play the doubleheader as planned.

"Mookie's handled this really well. We're kind of following his lead as far as trying to support him the best we can," Kershaw said. "It's been a difficult time. It's been a tough time for him personally, the Black community in general. Just trying to find different ways, what that looks like. It's new territory for us. We're trying to figure that out as well. The decision to play today, potentially continue to use our platform to speak out on things that shouldn't be happening and support Mookie in that and support the other Black baseball players, the whole Black community, I think is important."

Austin Barnes doubled in two runs to highlight the Dodgers' four-run fourth, when they also got RBI singles from Joc Pederson and Corey Seager.

NL-best Los Angeles (23-9) snapped San Francisco's seven-game winning streak. Giants starter Logan Webb (2-3) was done after 3 2/3 innings, tagged for five runs on four hits.

Clayton Kershaw
throws a pitch
during game 1 of
the doubleheader
between the Dodgers
and Giants.
BOB KUPBENS/
ICON SPORTSWIRE
VIA AP IMAGES

Joc Pederson is all smiles after a double during the doubleheader between the Dodgers and Giants.
BOB KUPBENS/ICON SPORTSWIRE VIA AP

Playoff Bound

Dodgers beat Padres 7-5 to clinch playoff spot

September 16, 2020

SAN DIEGO— While the Los Angeles Dodgers are regular participants in postseason baseball, there was something unusual about becoming the first team in the pandemic-shortened season to clinch a berth in the expanded playoffs.

"It's different, I guess. I just found that out five minutes ago," manager Dave Roberts said in his video news conference after the Dodgers beat the San Diego Padres 7-5 to take two of three in a matchup of the NL's two top teams.

The Dodgers opened a 3 1/2-game lead in their quest for an eighth straight NL West title by beating the Padres for the second straight day. Dustin May threw 5 1/3 gutty innings out of the bullpen, AJ Pollock and Chris Taylor homered and Will Smith drove in three runs.

"I'm celebrating by saying I'm proud of our guys and it was a great series," said Roberts, who grew up in northern San Diego County and both played for and was a coach with the Padres before getting the Dodgers' job. "I think it caught us all by surprise because we were so focused on trying to win this series. I think word will travel once we get on the plane."

San Diego, quieted by Dodgers pitching a second straight game even as it heads for its first playoff berth since winning the division in 2006, has lost two straight for the first time since mid-August.

May confirmed that as part of COVID-19 protocols, MLB doesn't want teams having wild clubhouse celebrations after clinching.

Asked if the Dodgers had a celebration, he said:

"No. We're not allowed to."

But clinching a postseason spot "is something you grind for all season long," he said. "This season is different but we had to grind in the quarantine zone, so you're still going to feel super excited."

At 35-15, the Dodgers breezed into the expanded 16-team postseason field. Los Angeles is seeking its first World Series title since 1988, having lost in the Fall Classic under Roberts in 2017 and 2018.

Mookie Betts tied his career high with three stolen bases, had two hits and scored a run.

San Diego, quieted by Dodgers pitching a second straight game even as it heads for its first playoff berth since winning the division in 2006, has lost two straight for the first time since mid-August.

"Today we just got beat in almost all areas, facets of the game," rookie manager Jayce Tingler said. "We didn't play as clean as we have been defensively. Their guys over there on the mound, they've done a good job pitching, especially the past two days. It was nice to scrap and crawl and fight back in it, but at the end of the day we got into too big a hole to overcome."

May, who had been scheduled to start before Roberts decided to go with a bullpen day, was the Dodgers' third pitcher of the game. He went 5 1/3 innings and was in control until Jurickson Profar homered to right field with two outs in the seventh to pull the Padres to 7-3. Mitch Moreland reached on an error by second baseman Gavin Lux opening the inning.

After Profar's homer, May struck out Trent Grisham and blew off some steam by yelling a few profanities that could be heard around empty Petco Park. Grisham angered the Dodgers by briefly posing at the plate after homering off Clayton Kershaw in the Padres' 7-2 win Monday night.

May allowed Manny Machado's solo homer with one out in the eighth, his 14th, and was lifted by Roberts.

Until the seventh, May had breezed through four innings by allowing only a single and a walk. He struck out six.

May said he felt his outing "was pretty solid. There were some miscues on my end that ended up going a pretty long ways. Just location-wise, it wasn't where I wanted on those two pitches and they took advantage of it."

Starter Brusdar Gasterol allowed a hit and a run in 1 1/3 innings before Adam Kolarek (3-0) allowed a hit and two walks in two-thirds of an inning.

Pedro Baez got the final two outs for his second save.

Facing: Relief pitcher Dustin May prepares to deliver a pitch during third inning action.
AP PHOTO/
DERRICK TUSKAN

Chris Taylor is congratulated by Dino Ebel after hitting a solo home run off Padres relief pitcher Garrett Richards.
AP PHOTO/DERRICK TUSKAN

Rocky Mountain High

September 18, 2020

Bellinger, Dodgers set season high for runs

DENVER — For his prodigious power, the 5-foot-9 Mookie Betts credits listening to his parents in the backyard.

"When I was a kid, 4 or 5 years old, mom and dad would always tell me hit it over their head," Betts explained.

He's been doing that to everyone ever since.

Betts hit his NL-leading 16th homer and the Los Angeles Dodgers set a season high for runs in their 15-6 romp past the Colorado Rockies to move closer to clinching their eighth straight NL West title.

The Dodgers' magic number for wrapping up the division dropped to four. They were already the first team to secure a playoff spot this season.

They're hitting their stride at the ideal time.

"You can't just turn it on at playoffs," Betts said. "You have to play throughout the season the same way you're going to play in the playoffs. ... We're doing a good job with that. We have to continue to do it."

Cody Bellinger had three of LA's season-high 17 hits, including his first homer since Aug. 30 and a double. He also added an RBI single as part of a five-run fifth inning that broke open the game.

"It's a huge night for him to get results," Dodgers manager Dave Roberts said. "I know he's going to sleep well tonight. Over the last few days, I think he's been swinging the bat better. I'm just happy to see him smiling and laughing."

Gavin Lux had a two-run homer in the second, while Betts delivered a solo shot in the sixth to increase the Dodgers' major league-leading homer total to 98. Every starter in the lineup had a hit and all but AJ Pollock scored a run.

"Everybody can hurt you," said Betts, who added a two-run triple in the seventh. "There's nobody you can say, 'OK, I'm going to attack this guy, pitch around this guy.' You'd pretty much have to pitch around everybody."

It was a bullpen game for the Dodgers, who started with Alex Wood and then used six relievers. Mitch White, who was recalled Friday, pitched two scoreless innings to earn his first big league win.

Josh Fuentes had a three-run homer for Colorado as part of his three-hit night. Fuentes, who's the cousin of Nolan Arenado, is hitting .339.

"With Josh, he's doing a lot of good things," Rockies manager Bud Black said. "He's coming to the park every day with a great winning attitude. It's really great to see."

Ryan Castellani (1-3) struggled with his command in allowing eight runs, seven earned, over 4 1/3 innings. He walked three and hit Austin Barnes in the back/neck area.

Colorado fell to 11-17 at Coors Field this season. With two games left, the team will finish below .500 at home for the ninth time in franchise history.

The team remains in the wild-card chase despite dropping five of its last six.

"The mood is one of frustration that we're not putting it all together," Black said. "We feel as though we're in a race with five, six teams that are battling for a couple spots and we're not getting it done."

Facing: Mookie Betts gestures to the dugout after he pulled into third base with a two-run triple off Rockies pitcher Wade Davis during the seventh inning.
AP PHOTO/
DAVID ZALUBOWSKI

Corey Seager swings at a pitch as Rockies catcher Tony Wolters prepares to catch the pitch from Ryan Castellani. Seager lined out on the at-bat.
AP PHOTO/DAVID ZALUBOWSKI

NL West Champs

Dodgers
clinch
NL West
title with
win over A's

September 22, 2020

Los Angeles — Wrapping up an NL West title has become routine for the Los Angeles Dodgers, but in a year in which no one was sure three months ago if there would be a baseball season, manager Dave Roberts wanted his team to still savor the moment.

The Dodgers clinched the NL's top postseason seed and eighth straight division title with a 7-2 victory over the Oakland Athletics. They are third team to win at least eight straight division titles, joining the Atlanta Braves (14 straight from 1991-2005) and New York Yankees (nine straight from 1998-2006).

"To fast forward a couple months and be crowned NL West champs is a credit to everyone. It should never be taken for granted," Roberts said. "Truth be told a lot of guys didn't know we could clinch. We were responsible but I let it know that it has to be appreciated."

The Dodgers, who own the best record in the majors at 39-16, were the first team in the majors to clinch a playoff berth on Sept. 16. They will open postseason play on Sept. 30 by hosting every game in a best-of-three series against the No. 8 seed.

Los Angeles came into the day with a magic number of two and got help with the Angels' 4-2 victory over the San Diego Padres.

Instead of a wild celebration on the mound after Jake McGee struck out Sean Murphy for the final out, players briskly walked out of the dugout to celebrate with teammates. Everyone grabbed a division clinching shirt and cap before heading to the mound for a group photo.

The clubhouse celebration was also muted. Champagne was still involved, but it was players toasting each other with a glass instead of being showered in it.

"We talked about it instead of dumping stuff on people. It's a moment you need to celebrate and we did," said Corey Seager, who had three hits and one of Los Angeles' four home runs, "It stinks not being able to do champagne and beer showers because some of the younger guys haven't been able to experience that."

Max Muncy, Chris Taylor and AJ Pollock also went deep for Los Angeles, which leads the majors with 104 home runs.

"This whole year has been weird. There's no other way to describe it," Muncy said. "It's sad not to be celebrate as usual but we know there is a lot more at stake."

Dustin May (2-1) went five innings and allowed two runs on three hits. The 22-year-old red-headed righty set a team record by not allowing more than three earned runs in his first 13 career starts, which include 10 this season.

Robbie Grossman homered for Oakland, which clinched its first AL West crown in seven years on Monday during a day off. The Athletics, in the postseason for the third straight year, currently are the AL's No. 3 seed.

Mark Canha had two of Oakland's five hits.

Seager tied it at 1 in the first with an RBI single and then led off the fifth with a drive to center off T.J. McFarland to extend LA's lead to 6-2.

Muncy gave the Dodgers a 3-2 lead in the third inning with a two-run homer. Taylor and Pollock extended it with solo shots in the fourth off Oakland starter Frankie Montas (3-5).

Grossman quickly gave Oakland a 1-0 lead when he homered off the left-field pole in the first inning. Sean Murphy briefly gave the Athletics a 2-1 advantage when he led off the third with a walk and scored on a wild pitch by May with two outs.

Montas, who allowed only four home runs in his first seven starts, has given up six in his past three. The right-hander went four innings and yielded five runs on seven hits with a walk and three strikeouts.

"They're a pretty good team that when you make mistakes, they make you pay," Oakland manager Bob Melvin said. "They're pretty good laying off and making you throw it over the plate. They made Montas pay, unfortunately."

Cody Bellinger added two hits for the Dodgers, including an RBI single with the bases loaded in the seventh.

Cody Bellinger slides safely into second with a double as Oakland shortstop Marcus Semien looks to apply the tag.
AP PHOTO/
ASHLEY LANDIS

The Dodgers pose for a photo after the team clinched the NL West title with a 7-2 win over the Athletics in Los Angeles.
AP PHOTO/ASHLEY LANDIS

Kings of LA

Pollock hits
2 HRs as
Dodgers blank
Angels 5-0

September 27, 2020

Los Angeles — AJ Pollock homered twice and the NL West champion Los Angeles Dodgers completed a three-game sweep of the Angels with a 5-0 victory to end the pandemic-shortened regular season.

Pollock's drive gave the Dodgers a major league-leading 118 homers. It was their fifth shutout victory; they went 15-1-4 in series this season.

The Dodgers won their eighth consecutive division title and finished 43-17 for the best record in the majors over the 60-game schedule. They were 106-56 last year playing a full 162 games. They'll open the postseason on Wednesday against Milwaukee at home.

"It's been a fun season," manager Dave Roberts said. "We can't wait until Wednesday. We feel we're the best team out there."

The Angels stumbled to a 26-34 mark. They were 72-90 last year, finishing fourth in the AL West, the same result as this season. They were 0-6 against the Dodgers, losing every game for the first time since 1997.

"They beat us up in kind of a heavyweight manner and it definitely indicates to us exactly where we need to get some work done moving to next year," said Joe Maddon, ending his first season in Anaheim as manager.

The Angels announced as the game ended that general manager Billy Eppler was fired after his fifth straight losing season.

Pollock started at leadoff in place of Mookie Betts, who is nursing a sore hip after getting plunked on Saturday. Pollock and Betts finished the season tied with a team-leading 16 homers.

"We have a lot of good power hitters on this team, not just Mookie," Pollock said. "I've had stretches where I've felt like the power has always been there, it's never really my goal. Just keep attacking the pitches I want to attack. If I do that, I know there's going to be some power numbers."

Joc Pederson singled leading off the seventh and Pollock followed with a two-run shot over the wall in center.

The Dodgers added two more runs in the third to make it 3-0. Austin Barnes walked and scored on Corey Seager's RBI groundout to second as part of a double play. Justin Turner popped up to right fielder Jared Walsh, who lost the ball in the sun for an error, scoring Pederson, who walked. Turner was safe at first.

The Angels were limited to three hits without slugger Mike Trout in the lineup. He took the last two days off.

Victor Gonzalez made his first career start for the Dodgers, tossing a scoreless inning with one strikeout before turning the ball over to Dustin May (3-1). The red-headed right-hander allowed two hits in four innings, struck out five and walked two.

Angels starter Patrick Sandoval (1-5) left the game with a strained left calf after giving up three straight walks that led to two runs with two outs in the third. The left-hander gave up three runs and one hit. He struck out three and walked three.

The Dodgers posted a message on the video boards thanking all the cardboard cutouts for their support. The team sold the cutouts with photos of fans on them and donated the proceeds to the club's foundation. Each of the cutouts was authenticated with a tiny sticker on the back.

At right: Corey Seager hustles into short left field to catch a fly ball.

Facing: A.J. Pollock with the swing that delivered one of his two home runs in the game.

AP PHOTOS/
KYUSUNG GONG

Justin Turner celebrates A.J. Pollock's solo home run during the first inning of a 5-0 win over the Angels.
AP PHOTO/KYUSUNG GONG

A Safe Bett

Trade for right fielder turns out to be a very smart move.

Someone once traded away Mookie Betts.

After the sense of awe dissipates following another spectacular play by the Los Angeles Dodgers' superstar right fielder, after the slow-motion replays confirm Betts's singular brilliance, after the thought is given to how outrageously fortunate the Dodgers are to have Betts in the fold as they make their march through the postseason to this week's World Series — after all that is dealt with and put aside, the mind inevitably returns to the same stunning, inconceivable realization:

Someone once had Mookie Betts on their team — and decided they would be better off with some other players instead.

That someone, of course, is the Boston Red Sox, whom Betts, the 2018 American League MVP, helped lead to the World Series title that fall — beating, of course, the Dodgers. It is now clear, if it wasn't at the time, that the trade eight months ago that sent Betts to the Dodgers along with pitcher David Price for a trio of younger players is the most consequential in recent baseball history — this generation's version of Frank Robinson for Milt Pappas.

"We would have beat the Red Sox" in 2018, Dodgers Manager Dave Roberts said in the aftermath of this season's NLCS Game 7 victory over the Atlanta Braves, "if we'd had Mookie Betts."

While the Red Sox have collapsed in on themselves — going from a championship in 2018 to a third-place finish in 2019 to last place in 2020, while undertaking an economic overhaul of which the Betts trade was the centerpiece — the Dodgers, with Betts as their indefatigable engine and franchise player, are preparing to face the Tampa Bay Rays in the World Series.

The Dodgers have several, complex reasons for believing this is the most complete of their eight-consecutive division-champion playoff teams, the first seven of which ended with October defeats: their enviable starting pitching depth, the many recent dividends of their player-development machine, the maturing of core players such as Corey Seager, Walker Buehler and Cody Bellinger.

But the simplest reason is this: Those teams didn't have Mookie Betts, and this one does.

"Mookie kind of separates himself, I think, with the consistency," said left-hander Clayton Kershaw, the Dodgers' longtime ace. "The other things he can do on the baseball field if he happens to not be getting hits — that's what separates him. There's also a confidence there — just a really calming influence. Thankfully, he's on our team."

The Dodgers knew what they were getting in Betts when they made the trade: a dynamic right fielder and hitter who can alter games with his glove, his bat, his legs or his arm. The 28-year-old hit .292 with 16 homers, slugged .562 and stole 10 bases during the truncated, 60-game regular season, playing defense like the four-time Gold Glove winner he is and lifting himself into the NL MVP conversation.

But there was more to Betts than even the Dodgers realized, and that, as much as the sheer, game-changing talent, was what prompted the Dodgers to sign Betts to a 12-year, $365 million contract extension in July. A franchise that is not prone to making blockbuster moves, and that had passed on one big free agent after another over the years — all in the name of future economic flexibility — had decided, for once, to go all-in. Betts made the Dodgers change course.

"It's incredible what he does on defense, what he does on the bases, in the batter's box," Dodgers president of baseball operations Andrew Friedman told reporters during a video interview. "The instincts and feel for the game are usually seen in extra players — because they have to do those extra things to get to the big leagues and stick around. You rarely see that in the best player on the field."

"I love the coaching staff, the players, the front office," Betts said of his first season in L.A. On Oct. 5, at the end of their workout on the eve of the division series against the San Diego Padres, the Dodgers huddled in the outfield at Globe Life Field. Two players spoke to the group. The first was third baseman Justin Turner, the Dodgers' longest-tenured position player. The second was Betts, their newest. What Betts lacked in Dodgers tenure, he more than made up for in stature.

"We talked about it leading up to it," Turner said of him and Betts. "Just address the team, make sure everyone is on the same page. It's obvious we all know what's at stake and what we're playing for — but just [to] remind the guys not everything is always going to go our way. It might not always be easy. But as long as we keep mentally grinding, support each other and play together as a group, we'll get through anything."

Betts backed up his words with his play. He went 3 for 7 with three doubles and drove in three of the Dodgers' seven runs in a two-game mini-sweep of the Milwaukee Brewers in the first round, then went 4 for 12 with two more doubles in a three-game sweep of the Padres.

Organizations spend millions of dollars, scouts sort through thousands of prospects, and front offices devote hours and days and months and years to the mission of locating, nurturing and deploying a player such as Mookie Betts. If you're lucky, you find one like him in a lifetime.

The Dodgers have Betts on their side. It is good to be them — especially now, entering the World Series. But someone else had him and then sent him away. Hard to imagine.

Right fielder Mookie Betts signed a 12-year, $365 million contract extension in July.
PHOTO BY BRIAN ROTHMULLER/ICON SPORTSWIRE

The Good Doctor

"Everybody's aware of the drought. The fans are itching for the championship. Everybody trusts Doc. We're working hard to bring home a championship for him and the city of L.A."

— DODGERS CATCHER AUSTIN BARNES

No one in the World Series is under more pressure than Dave Roberts. The only acceptable outcome for him is to manage the Los Angeles Dodgers to a championship.

The Dodgers had a chance in 2017 and fell to the nefarious Houston Astros. They returned in 2018 and lost again to the steamroller Red Sox.

The Washington Nationals upset the 106-win Dodgers in the Division Series last season, bringing more heat on Roberts. But the team was quick to say he would return.

If the gilded Dodgers can't beat the Tampa Bay Rays this year, Roberts may not get another chance. The Dodgers are so loaded with talent that the blame will fall on the manager, fairly or not.

Roberts understands October tension.

"I think it's just more understanding the great fan bases and what it means to them [to win it all]," Roberts said before Game 3 of the World Series. "When you take on this job with a team that hasn't won in a long time, that's part of it. That comes with the job.

"I take it as the passion and care of the fans. I want it for all of us."

A speedy outfielder selected by the Tigers in the 28th round of the 1994 amateur draft, Roberts began his big-league career with the Indians in 1999, Cleveland's 51st consecutive season without winning it all. He concluded his run with the Giants in 2008, that franchise's 54th straight campaign without standing last. The Giants ended their drought two years later, and then again in 2012 and 2014; the Indians are still trying, their 72-year run the longest in any North American professional sport.

In between those stints, Roberts played for the Red Sox in 2004, their 86th try at ending the alleged Curse of the Bambino. The drought ended right there and then in no small part due to Roberts' ninth-inning steal of second base during American League Championship Series Game 4 against the Yankees, which sparked the historic comeback that culminated in Boston's World Series victory over the Cardinals.

"I don't think there could be any more than what we dealt with in Boston," Roberts said. "That was a lot of burden to inherit."

Asked whether he thought those collective burdens enabled him to deal with the narrative surrounding the Dodgers, who last won the World Series in 1988 (this marks their 14th postseason appearance since then), Roberts, known to most of his players as "Doc," said, "I think so."

"Everybody's aware of the drought in L.A. The fans are itching for the championship," Dodgers catcher Austin Barnes said before the World Series. "We're working hard to bring home a championship for Doc and for the city of L.A."

Think of those Indians teams in the mid-to-late 1990s that fielded those fearsome lineups — Albert Belle, Manny Ramirez, Jim Thome and more — yet couldn't finish the job. Or the Giants' long run of relevance under Dusty Baker and Felipe Alou continually falling short before they undertook a rebuilding that led them to their mini-dynasty. This game ain't easy and keeps getting harder. You need every advantage you can find.

No manager will be perfect. Roberts, however, might just possess a set of particular experiences that makes him an optimal guy to appease the good folks of Southern California.

"The way he has trust in the clubhouse, everybody trusts Doc," Barnes said. "He's very personable with everybody. We've been through the grind with each other."

Thirty-two years can be quite a grind for a fan base, yet it could be far worse. And Roberts knows that.

"If we can keep our guys focused on ourselves and playing good baseball," Roberts said. "I just believe that if we can do that throughout the playoffs, we're the best team and we should ultimately accomplish our goal."

Facing: Dave Roberts watches batting practice before Game 6 of the NLCS.
AP PHOTO/SUE OGROCKI

A Star on the Rise

Seager's
swings strike
fear in the
heart of
opponents

I t's a lineup that features the reigning National League MVP and another star that recently signed a $365 million contract extension. Yet the Dodgers' best offensive player probably isn't Cody Bellinger or Mookie Betts.

Enter Corey Seager, the 26-year-old shortstop whose raw talent has been on display throughout this postseason. The fact the Dodgers reached the World Series, after avoiding elimination from the NLCS against the Atlanta Braves, was partly a function of Seager's dangerous left-handed bat.

He entered Game 6 of the NLCS with four homers and 10 RBIs in the series. Included was two homers Friday night that helped bump his slash line for this postseason to .342/.409/.842.

"I didn't know much before I came over," Betts said, referring to Seager. "I just knew he was a good shortstop who could swing it a little bit. And getting to see him day in and day out is definitely a blessing. I have really one job: to get on base and stay there until he hits me in, which doesn't take too long."

It's a different Seager than the Dodgers had seen in previous Octobers. Before this year, Seager had appeared in 31 postseason games and owned a disappointing .203/.275/.331 slash line. Now he's among a list of players that includes Giancarlo Stanton (2020), Nelson Cruz (2011), B.J. Upton (2008) and Jim Thome (1999) who have at least four homers and 10 RBIs in a postseason series.

But Seager doesn't want to hear about his own accomplishments at this point.

"The whole goal is to win, we haven't done that yet," he said. "So regardless of what you're doing, if you don't win at the end of the year, it's not the same. We're just trying to win a game and let things happen."

"I'm just putting good swings on good pitches right now. And everything is kind of clicking."

Seager missed most of 2018 — which included a second straight World Series appearance for the Dodgers — after undergoing in-season Tommy John surgery. He returned the following year, played through hip discomfort that led to surgery near the end of the season and led the NL in doubles with 44, but he didn't have a real breakout until 2020.

In the 60-game sprint, Seager hit .307/.358/.585 with 15 homers and 41 RBIs.

"He's healthy, he's been healthy, he's had a tremendous year, the experience he's had in the postseason — all of it is lining up right now," Dodgers manager Dave Roberts said. "For me, there's no better player."

Seager's homers Friday included a blast leading off the fourth that cut the Braves' lead to 2-1. In the seventh, after Will Smith's three-run homer put the Dodgers ahead for the first time, Seager homered again.

Justin Turner is the only other player in franchise history with 14 RBIs in one postseason.

"[Seager] is something else," Braves manager Brian Snitker said. "He's one of those guys who never gives an at-bat away. It's very impressive. He's a dangerous, impressive hitter."

Dodgers shortstop Corey Seager throws to first to get an out during a game against the Mariners in August.
AP PHOTO/ALEX GALLARDO

October Red

"He's the glue for our club. If you're talking about the grind, the tough conversations, the identity of our ballclub, he's the face. He personifies everything that I believe in as a baseball player."
— DODGERS MANAGER
DAVE ROBERTS
ON JUSTIN TURNER

Facing: Justin Turner is recognizable not only for his red hair and bushy beard, but also for the stain of pine tar on the back of his jersey.
PHOTO BY KYUSUNG
GONG/ICON SPORTSWIRE

The bushy beard, the pine tar stain on the back of his No. 10 Los Angeles Dodgers jersey and all of those postseason hits.

That's October Red.

Justin Turner is one of the constants for the Dodgers during their third World Series in four years, and his Duke Snider-matching homer in the first inning of Game 3 of the World Series put them ahead to stay on way to a 6-2 win for a 2-1 series lead over Tampa Bay — and halfway to their first championship since 1988.

A month shy of turning 36, the beloved Turner also scored after a double and showed off a nifty glove at third base.

That stain created by aggressive practice swings may cover half of his name on his back, but he is a very familiar figure in October — this was his 15th World Series game.

Turner, who grew up in Long Beach and played at Cal State Fullerton, earlier this month passed Steve Garvey for the most postseason hits in franchise history. His solo shot in the first off Charlie Morton matched the 11 homers hit by Snider — the Hall of Fame center fielder who played for Dodgers World Series championship teams in Brooklyn and Los Angeles. Turner's 40 RBIs are Dodgers postseason record.

All of the postseason homers for Turner have come in the past five seasons. Only Nelson Cruz (17) and Jim Edmonds (13) have hit more homers in the postseason after turning 30, after none before that.

His record 18th postseason double came in the third before scoring on Max Muncy's two-run single for a 3-0 lead. Turner had a couple of fine plays in the bottom half, stepping back to field a hard grounder and making a strong throw to retire Willy Adames, then reaching up to grab a hot chopper that started an inning-end double play.

And those came when the versatile infielder wasn't roaming around during the various defensive shifts incorporated by the Dodgers. He is often on the move after two strikes, venturing from closer to third base to the other side of second.

While he was hitting only .216 since the end of the regular season going into Game 3, Turner went 2 for 5 to extend his postseason on-base streak to 11 in a row.

Turner has 75 hits in 69 postseason games, all with the Dodgers since 2014 after joining the team as a free agent.

That came after he hit .307 in the regular season, which he ended by reaching base safely in 31 consecutive games with a plate appearance— his career long, and the second-longest in the majors this year behind the 33 in a row by Atlanta's Freddie Freeman.

Turner is at the end of a $64 million, four-year contract he got in free agency to re-sign for the Dodgers before the current run of World Series. He has been part of seven of their eight consecutive NL West titles.

Is there an added sense of urgency to get a World Series ring with his career winding down?

"I think it's the same urgency as every season," Turner said before the start of the World Series. "When we show up to Arizona in spring training, the goal is to win a World Series, and nothing has changed this season. We have a lot of guys with a lot of experience who are all just as hungry, just as eager as I am.

"I try to stay in the present. When you look ahead to the future you can destroy your focus. So I try not to do that. I try to worry about today, and when tomorrow comes, I'll worry about tomorrow."

Big Hits When They Count

Seager
homers,
Dodgers win
wild-card
opener

Oct 1, 2020

LOS ANGELES — The Los Angeles Dodgers' powerful lineup went mostly quiet against the Milwaukee Brewers. Still, baseball's best team in the regular season generated just enough offense and got plenty of help from the opposing pitcher.

Mookie Betts had two hits and an RBI and Corey Seager homered in the Dodgers' 4-2 victory in the opener of their NL playoff Wednesday night.

The eight-time NL West champion Dodgers capitalized early in a bullpen game for the Brewers and can wrap up the best-of-three series Thursday. Milwaukee -- a playoff entrant despite a losing record -- limped into the postseason as the No. 8 seed without its best starter and reliever, who are hurt.

"A walk is just as good as a hit sometimes, which we showed in the first inning," Seager said. "You don't always have to have the big hit to score runs."

The Dodgers took a 2-0 lead on a leadoff double by Betts and four walks by left-hander Brent Suter in the first, tying for the most walks by a pitcher in a single inning in postseason history. Betts scored when Will Smith drew a four-pitch walk with the bases loaded. Seager walked and scored on AJ Pollock's bases-loaded walk.

"We took our walks and scratched out some runs," said Seager, who hit just behind Betts.

Dodgers manager Dave Roberts said, "You'd be hard-pressed to find a better 1-2 in baseball."

Suter needed 32 pitches to get out of the inning. He gave up three runs and three hits in 1 2/3 innings. He doubled his season total of five walks, and he didn't record a strikeout.

"Nerves going on, excited to be out there, then Mookie gets that leadoff double. I missed some corners, then all of a sudden snowball effect," Suter said. "I felt like I let the team down big-time."

Chris Taylor doubled leading off the second and scored on Betts' double, making it 3-0. Max Muncy walked with two outs and Ryan Braun caught Smith's drive to right at the wall to end the inning, potentially saving three runs.

Braun winced as he hit the wall with his right shoulder. He left in the fifth with mid-back discomfort.

"He hurt himself Sunday in St. Louis and we tried to give it a shot today and at some point it was a no-go," Brewers manager Craig Counsell said. "You could call it day-to-day."

The Dodgers could have inflicted more damage but were just 1 for 7 with runners in scoring position in the first two innings.

Milwaukee pitchers retired 10 straight Dodgers during one stretch.

With the Dodgers clinging to a one-run lead in the seventh, Seager went deep to straightaway center off Freddy Peralta, who gave up just two homers during the shortened 60-game season. The Dodgers led the majors with 118 homers.

Los Angeles closer Kenley Jansen walked pinch-hitter Jace Peterson with two outs in the ninth. Christian Yelich came to the plate as the potential tying run, but he struck out swinging to end the game. Jansen earned the save.

"Despite pitching about as bad as I've ever pitched, we still had a chance to win," Suter said.

The Brewers closed to 3-2 on Orlando Arcia's two-strike, two-run homer with two outs in the fourth. Betts made an over-the-shoulder catch to deny Avisail Garcia with a runner on for the second out of the inning.

Milwaukee had the potential tying run on in the seventh with Yelich's two-out double. Tyrone Taylor popped up to end the inning.

The Brewers also threatened in the sixth. Garcia singled and was safe at second on Muncy's fielding error at first base. Muncy turned and scrambled into short right, trying to pick up the ball with a swooping motion, but it went off his glove and rolled away.

Julio Urias retired the next two batters to end the inning.

"We gave ourselves a shot," Counsell said. "We just didn't come through."

Urias got the victory, allowing three hits in three innings and striking out five. He had a runner on base in each of his innings, but didn't allow a run.

Garcia had three hits and Yelich two to lead the Brewers.

Pitching with a blister on his right index finger, Walker Buehler allowed two runs and three hits in four innings for Los Angeles. He struck out eight and walked two.

Roberts pulled Buehler once he got over 20 pitches in the fourth.

"At that point in time is when the blister starts to show itself a little bit," Roberts said. "We just didn't know what we were going to get from Walker."

Facing: Mookie Betts delivers one of his two hits during Game 1 of the wild-card series in Los Angeles.
AP PHOTO/
ASHLEY LANDIS

Dodger Stadium is seen without fans as the
national anthem is played before Game 1 of
a National League wild-card series.
AP PHOTO/ASHLEY LANDIS

Dodgers Draw an Ace

Kershaw
Blanks
Brewers 3-0

Oct 2, 2020

LOS ANGELES — Beat up in the postseason over the years, Clayton Kershaw orchestrated one of his best performances against the weakened Milwaukee Brewers.

Kershaw struck out 13 while delivering eight innings of three-hit ball, Mookie Betts hit a two-out, two-run double in the fifth, and the Los Angeles Dodgers won 3-0 to sweep their NL wild-card series on Thursday night.

"This was a fun night for me," said Kershaw, who displayed a rare smile on the mound. "Get the postseason off to a good start. It's a good first step for sure."

The eight-time West champion Dodgers advanced to the NL Division Series in Arlington, Texas, and will play either the St. Louis Cardinals or San Diego Padres, who meet in a deciding Game 3 on Friday.

Kershaw's strikeouts were a playoff career high and the most by a Dodgers pitcher in the postseason since his mentor Sandy Koufax had 15 in Game 1 of the 1963 World Series against the Yankees.

"That was pretty spectacular, for sure," Betts said. "He gave us all the opportunities in the world to capitalize."

Kershaw issued his lone walk to Luis Urias in the eighth and promptly picked him off when a diving Urias couldn't get back to the bag. The Brewers lost their challenge of the call.

"Kershaw was just determined," Dodgers manager Dave Roberts said. "He gave us all he had and all we needed."

Kershaw, a three-time NL Cy Young Award winner, showed none of the fallibility that's plagued his postseason career. He came in with a 9-11 record and 4.43 ERA in the playoffs. A year ago, he came on in relief of starter Walker Buehler against Washington, gave up back-to-back homers and was removed in Game 5 of the Division Series.

This time, he had his way with the beleaguered Brewers. He gave up singles to Jedd Gyorko, Urias and Keston Hiura.

"Offensively, it was a struggle," Brewers manager Craig Counsell said. "Kershaw, he was exceptional. His slider was as good as I remember it."

Neither team managed to hit a ball hard as Brandon Woodruff and Kershaw dueled through four innings. Only two of the Dodgers' nine hitters didn't strike out during that span; five of the Brewers didn't.

After leading the majors with 118 home runs this season, Los Angeles managed just one hit through four innings, a single by Austin Barnes, before breaking out in the fifth with a trio of singles.

Cody Bellinger and Chris Taylor had back-to-back singles up the middle with one out. AJ Pollock grounded into a fielder's choice to third and Urias stepped on the bag to force Bellinger and fired to first. But Gyorko couldn't handle the throw in time to complete the double play.

"It's a difficult play. We just didn't make it," Counsell said, "and it ended up costing us because they're a good team."

Barnes singled with two outs to set up Betts, who doubled sharply down the third-base line. The ball rolled into the left-field corner and three runs scored to chase Woodruff.

Woodruff allowed three runs and five hits in 4 2/3 innings. The right-hander struck out a career postseason high of nine against no walks. As he was walking off the mound after being replaced, Woodruff shouted expletives and gestured angrily in the direction of plate umpire Quinn Wolcott, who tossed him. Woodruff grew upset when a 1-2 pitch to Barnes was called a ball.

"I thought it was a strike," Woodruff said. "Just the heat of the moment and really wanting to put up a zero, at that moment I knew that that could have been a big turning point with that call. That's why the reaction was what it was."

Brusdar Graterol pitched the ninth to earn his first career save for the Dodgers, with veteran closer Kenley Jansen watching from the bullpen. Graterol allowed a single, the Brewers' fourth hit of the game.

Milwaukee never got above .500 all season and posted a losing record before eking into the expanded postseason as the No. 8 seed.

"Every time your season comes to an end, it's a bummer," said Christian Yelich, who was 0 for 4 with two strikeouts. "It's a bummer because it's never the same team the next year. We went through a lot as a group. I'm definitely proud of the guys."

The Dodgers had the best record in baseball at 43-17 during the shortened 60-game season, and earned home-field advantage throughout the postseason. But from here on out, they'll be playing their games in Texas. That's where the NL Division Series and NL Championship Series will be contested, as well as the first neutral site World Series.

Facing: Dodgers starter Clayton Kershaw throws to a Milwaukee batter during the first inning of Game 2.
AP PHOTO/
ASHLEY LANDIS

Chris Taylor scores on a single by teammate
Austin Barnes in the fifth inning of Game 2.
KEITH BIRMINGHAM/THE ORANGE COUNTY REGISTER VIA AP

Walk in a New Park

Dodgers open
NLDS with win
over Padres

Oct 7, 2020

ARLINGTON, TEXAS — Justin Turner and the Los Angeles Dodgers had a walk in the new park to start their National League Division Series.

The patient Dodgers had already drawn nine free passes before Mookie Betts got their first hit in the sixth inning, and they went ahead to stay on Corey Seager's sacrifice fly right after that in a 5-1 win over the NL West rival San Diego Padres.

"We didn't get a lot of hits early, but we took great at-bats and we made those guys work," said Turner, who drew two bases on balls. "Our offense is at its best when we're walking as many times as we're getting hits."

Mike Clevinger made it only two pitches into the second inning of his postseason debut for the Padres before leaving with the same elbow injury that sidelined him during the first round. San Diego's heavily worked bullpen couldn't keep putting up zeros -- or keeping runners off base, even though the Padres gave up only four hits.

Game 2 in the best-of-five series at the Texas Rangers' new ballpark is Wednesday night.

When Chris Taylor, the No. 9 batter in the Los Angeles order, walked with one out in the sixth in a 1-1 game, it was the Dodgers' ninth walk through 27 batters and the Padres were already on their sixth pitcher. Betts then doubled into the left-field corner to break up the no-hitter, sending Taylor to third and setting up Seager's sac fly.

"We felt like it was a matter of time," Cody Bellinger said. "We grinded, and it was a good team win."

Los Angeles got all its hits in the sixth, including RBI singles by Turner and Bellinger. Another run scored on a wild pitch and the Dodgers also drew their 10th walk, matching Atlanta in 1997 for the most in a nine-inning NLDS game.

The Dodgers scored an unearned run in the fourth when Bellinger reached on a two-out throwing error by rookie second baseman Jake Cronenworth after two walks and a wild pitch earlier in the inning.

Dustin May (1-0), the 23-year-old Dodgers right-hander who grew up about 30 miles away in Justin, Texas, struck out three over two perfect innings in relief of Walker Buehler. Kenley Jansen, the fourth reliever, finished a three-hitter for Los Angeles.

Garrett Richards (0-1) was gone after giving up the hit to Betts. So was rookie manager Jayce Tingler, who was ejected by plate umpire Lance Barrett for arguing balls and strikes when making yet another pitching change.

"Bottom line, we lost the battle of the strike zone on both sides," Tingler said. "We know they're a disciplined team, and they didn't chase. At the same time, we had chances offensively and they made some big pitches to get out of some jams."

With injured starters Clevinger and Dinelson Lamet out for the first round, the Padres became the first team to use at least eight pitchers in three consecutive playoff games. Nine relievers combined on a four-hit shutout in the Game 3 clincher over the St. Louis Cardinals last Friday.

The nine pitchers in a nine-inning game is a postseason record, and the Padres have now done it three times in four games.

Clevinger left his last regular-season start Sept. 23 after one inning because of an elbow impingement, but was added to the Padres' 28-player NLDS roster earlier Tuesday, when he was named the starter for Game 1. The herky-jerky right-hander, acquired from Cleveland in a nine-player trade Aug. 31, walked two and threw a wild pitch in a scoreless first.

After Clevinger went 2-0 on Bellinger to start the second, Tingler and a trainer visited the mound, and the pitcher left after a brief conversation. It was only his second start start since a two-hit shutout in a seven-inning complete game Sept. 13.

Buehler struck out eight, but the right-hander who has dealt with blisters all year needed a season-high 95 pitches to get through four innings. He walked four and allowed only two singles.

That included Austin Nola's two-out RBI single in the fourth that drove home Wil Myers, who walked before stealing second base.

In the stadium where the Padres began their record streak of grand slams in four consecutive games, Buehler walked the bases loaded with one out in the second inning. Buehler got out of the jam with strikeouts of Jurickson Profar and leadoff hitter Trent Grisham, but finished that inning already with 53 pitches and more balls than strikes (27-26).

Walker Buehler throws during the first inning of the NLDS game against San Diego.
AP PHOTO/ TONY GUTIERREZ)

Enrique Hernandez celebrates after Justin Turner scored on a hit by Cody Bellinger during the sixth inning in Game 1.
AP PHOTO/SUE OGROCKI

A Perfect Snare

Bellinger robs
Padres as
Dodgers hold
on for 2-0
NLDS lead

Oct 8, 2020

ARLINGTON, TEXAS —- Cody Bellinger would take the homer-robbing catch over the home run he hit if he had to pick from the two. The Los Angeles Dodgers needed both from their MVP center fielder.

Bellinger nearly went to a knee to hit his long home run, and later made a spectacular, leaping catch at the center-field wall to take away a go-ahead shot from Fernando Tatis Jr. as the Dodgers barely held off the San Diego Padres 6-5 Wednesday night.

Los Angeles took a 2-0 lead in the NL Division Series when Joe Kelly finally got the last out with the bases loaded in a tension-filled ninth inning.

"It's going to take a while to wind down from that one," said Bellinger, the 2019 NL MVP. "That's postseason baseball right there."

Kelly retired Eric Hosmer on a routine grounder to earn the save after Dodgers All-Star closer Kenley Jansen wobbled in the ninth. Los Angeles can sweep the best-of-five set from its NL West rival Thursday night.

The Padres were down one with a runner on and two outs in the seventh when Tatis, the 21-year-old budding superstar, hit a towering drive to center. Bellinger ran nearly 100 feet while watching the ball, then jumped and extended his gloved right hand above the 8-foot wall to make the grab.

"I just kind of turned around as fast as I could, got to the fence and saw that it was probable, so I decided to try to time up the jump, and it's how it worked out," Bellinger said. "I didn't know if it was a homer or not, but I knew I caught it."

Brusdar Graterol, the second Dodgers reliever after starter Clayton Kershaw, slung his glove and cap away and thrust both arms into the air to celebrate. Graterol also appeared to wave goodbye and blow a kiss at Padres star Manny Machado, who shouted curses back from afar in a heated verbal exchange that included other Dodgers as well.

Bellinger said it was only the second homer he has robbed in his career -- the first in the playoffs.

"Certainly turned out being the difference in the game," Padres rookie manager Jayce Tingler said. "Tatis squared it up pretty good. For him to go up and rob one there, there's not much to say."

Game 3 is Thursday night, and the Dodgers can advance to the NL Championship Series for the fourth time in five seasons. They went to the World Series in 2017 and 2018 before losing in a five-game Division Series to the Washington Nationals last October.

Corey Seager put the NL West champions ahead to stay with his two-run double in the third and scored on the first of Max Muncy's two RBI singles in the game. Leading off the next inning, Bellinger went after a low pitch and drove it 433 feet to center to make it 4-1.

Kershaw followed up his gem in the clinching game of the first round against Milwaukee with six strikeouts and no walks over six solid innings to get the win. The lefty allowed three runs, including back-to-back solo homers by Machado and Hosmer in the sixth, in his first start near his Texas home in a 13-season career.

After issuing full-count walks with two outs to Tatis and Machado that loaded the bases, Kelly retired Hosmer on a groundout for his first save this postseason. Jansen had allowed two runs in the ninth, on a pinch-hit RBI double by Mitch Moreland before he scored on Trent Grisham's single.

"Never a doubt — we had it in our hands. That's how Joe Kelly rolls. Joe likes to make it interesting for us," Kershaw said.

Zach Davies allowed four runs over five innings, the longest outing by a Padres pitcher in their five games this postseason. The right-hander struck out three without a walk but took the loss.

Three-time NL Cy Young Award winner Kershaw grew up, went to high school and still lives about 25 miles from the Texas Rangers' new stadium. The Dodgers have played four regular-season series in Arlington since his big league debut in 2008, but none of those matched up with his turn in the rotation.

Kershaw could pitch there more this October, since the NL Championship and World Series will also be played in the $1.2 billion ballpark with a retractable roof that has been open for the NLDS.

The Padres took a 1-0 lead in the second when Tommy Pham blooped a single just over the infield, and scored when Wil Myers lined a double into the right-center gap.

Seager's go-ahead double landed just fair down the right-field line, then ricocheted off the screen fronting the field-level club where Dodgers family members sat. The ball shot sideways away from right fielder Myers, allowing catcher Austin Barnes to score from first.

When the Dodgers went to bat after Bellinger's catch, Justin Turner had a sacrifice fly and Muncy his second RBI single to make it 6-3.

Facing: Cody Bellinger goes up high over the wall to steal the go-ahead home run from the Padres' Fernando Tatis Jr. in Game 2.
AP PHOTO/
TONY GUTIERREZ

BLUE HEAVEN

Corey Seager watches the flight of his two-RBI double off Padres pitcher Zach Davies during the third inning.
AP PHOTO/SUE OGROCKI

How Sweep It Is

Dodgers crush
Padres, move
on to the
NLCS

Oct 9, 2020

ARLINGTON, TEXAS — Justin Turner and the Los Angeles Dodgers have completed the first step of what they hope is a long stay in the Lone Star State.

Turner put the Dodgers ahead with a record-breaking hit in a big inning fueled by a nice stop-gone-bad by Fernando Tatis Jr., and they closed out a three-game NL Division Series sweep of the San Diego Padres with an 12-3 win Thursday night.

"Records are cool, championships are better," said Turner, who was part of the 2017 and 2018 National League championship teams that fell short in the World Series. "Until you're the last team standing, that's the ultimate goal."

Will Smith set a Dodgers postseason record with five hits, and Joc Pederson had a two-run single to cap that decisive five-run third as Los Angeles advanced to its fourth NL Championship Series in five years. The Dodgers lost to the Washington Nationals in a five-game division series last season.

After earning a spot in their 14th NLCS, to match the St. Louis Cardinals for the most, the Dodgers gathered for a team picture on the pitcher's mound at the same ballpark where the NLCS and World Series will be played.

"We obviously feel really confident about our club, we've still got a lot to work to do though," AJ Pollock said. "We did what we wanted to do, we did what we're supposed to do. We're going to celebrate that, but we expected it."

Turner's RBI single made it 3-2 and was his 64th career postseason hit, breaking a tie with Steve Garvey for the most in Dodgers postseason history.

That came right after Tatis, the 21-year-old budding superstar, made a diving play on Corey Seager's hard grounder, but then tried to make a throw from his knee. The ball skipped along the dirt and past first baseman Eric Hosmer, allowing Mookie Betts to score the tying run.

After 2019 NL MVP Cody Bellinger was intentionally walked with two outs after already having a 2-0 count, Pollock drove home Turner with a single, and Pederson lined his single over the outstretched glove of third baseman Manny Machado to make it 6-2.

Smith delivered an RBI single in the fourth and a two-run double in the ninth off the 11th Padres pitcher -- a postseason record. Betts, a day after his 28th birthday and signed for 12 more years, scored three times and had a sacrifice fly.

"Our offense was great. We had big plays, big moments from a lot of different guys throughout the series," Pollock said.

The Dodgers open the best-of-seven NLCS on Monday in the Texas Rangers' new $1.2 billion stadium with a retractable roof. They face Atlanta with fans in attendance for the first time during this pandemic-altered season.

Julio Urias (2-0), the third Dodgers pitcher, struck out six, walked one and allowed an unearned run over his five innings.

Garvey went to three World Series with the Dodgers and was part of their 1981 title. Three years later, he was with the Padres for their first World Series appearance.

Tatis, Machado and these Padres, who got only one inning out of injured Mike Clevinger this postseason and were also without their other top starter Dinelson Lamet, will have to wait until next season for another chance to overtake the Dodgers.

"They outplayed us. They played better baseball than we did," Tatis said. "We've just got to learn. This is just getting started."

The Padres loaded the bases in the bottom of the second, but there would be no more grand slams -- not like in the four games in a row they hit those against the Rangers, including their only two previous games at Globe Life Field. That slam streak was part of seven wins in a row that pushed San Diego into second place in the NL West, where it stayed and finished six games behind the Dodgers.

"Their pitching staff over there was really good," Padres rookie manager Jayce Tingler said. "We had a couple of opportunities to strike when we had some baserunners on. It seems like when we got to those positions, that's when their guys beared down and made some pitches."

San Diego did take a 2-1 lead, on rookie Jake Cronenworth's walk after Wil Myers was intentionally walked to load the bases with two outs, and Trent Grisham's RBI single before Tatis struck out.

Facing: Will Smith
follows through on
a single during thie
eighth inning of
Game 3.
AP PHOTO/
SUE OGROCKI

First Bump in the Road

Bullpen falters as Braves take NLCS opener

October 13, 2020

ARLINGTON, TEXAS — Walker Buehler is dealing with two blisters, and the Los Angeles Dodgers are having trouble settling on even one closer.

As for the offense, this wasn't the blistering start the Dodgers wanted.

Blake Treinen surrendered Austin Riley's tiebreaking homer leading off the ninth, and the last 13 LA batters of the game were retired in Atlanta's 5-1 victory in the NL Championship Series opener Monday night.

Treinen and lefty Jake McGee combined to give up four runs in the ninth, while Kenley Jansen never saw the mound as the club's career leader in saves struggles with velocity and command. Manager Dave Roberts has chosen his words carefully while saying the bullpen roles are open in the ninth.

"I just felt that in a tie ballgame right there, us the home team, I just felt that that run right there was really good for Blake," Roberts said. "He's going to have to do it again. It just didn't work out."

Ronald Acuña Jr. followed Riley's homer with a double, and Treinen was gone after giving up Marcell Ozuna's RBI single. Treinen's only out was a long flyball to center by Freddie Freeman that moved Ozuna to third. McGee gave up Ozzie Albies' two-run homer.

Roberts said after the game Buehler has been dealing with two blisters, but the right-hander still pitched into the sixth inning for the first time this postseason despite a career-high five walks. He threw a season-high 100 pitches.

"It's hard to say you're too fine," Buehler said. "I feel like I've been decently successful. I don't want to walk guys. We're trying to keep runs off the board. I can go deeper. I can be better."

Enrique Hernandez watches his home run against the Atlanta Braves during the fifth inning.
AP PHOTO/SUE OGROCKI

Buehler allowed one run with seven strikeouts in five innings, leaving after allowing consecutive singles to Travis d'Árnaud and Albies to start the sixth.

"Over the last month there's been kind of two blister situations and they kind of take turns," Roberts said. "But I do feel we came out well today."

Brusdar Graterol replaced Buehler and retired three straight to escape the sixth. Dustin May and Víctor González combined for two scoreless innings, with González striking out Charlie Culberson with the bases loaded to end the eighth.

Baseball's highest-scoring offense was no match for the hottest playoff pitching staff.

The Dodgers didn't have a baserunner over the final four innings. The last to reach was Corey Seager via single, three batters after Kiké Hernández's solo home run leading off the fifth. The other three hits for the Dodgers, who led the majors in homers during the regular season, were singles.

Atlanta, the first team since the 1905 New York Giants to record four shutouts in the first five games in the same postseason, remained unbeaten in the playoffs while handing LA its first loss.

"Their energy was a little bit better than ours tonight," Hernández said. "They came right out of the gates. We'll throw this one away and come back tomorrow with a fresh mind."

Victor Gonzalez celebrates striking out the Braves' Charlie Culberson with the bases loaded during the eighth inning.
AP PHOTO/ERIC GAY

Dodgers fans watch from their cars during a drive-in viewing party for Game 1 of the National League Championship Series in the Dodgers Stadium parking lot.
KIRBY LEE VIA AP

Braves Look in Command

Dodgers in deep hole down 0-2

October 13, 2020

ARLINGTON, TEXAS — Former ace Clayton Kershaw is having more back issues, Kenley Jansen hasn't seen the mound yet with his closing role unclear and baseball's highest-scoring offense stayed silent until it was too late.

It's no wonder the Los Angeles Dodgers are down 2-0 in the NL Championship Series to the Atlanta Braves, a deficit the previous 14 NL teams to face in the best-of-seven format couldn't overcome.

The Dodgers, who won their first five playoff games before dropping their second straight 8-7 on Tuesday night, can't get in gear in the first neutral-site NLCS and could be headed to 32 years and counting since their last championship.

Los Angeles trails 2-0 in an NLCS for the first time since 2013, when it lost in six games to St. Louis. The Dodgers have returned to the postseason every year since, finishing short of a title each time.

At least LA showed some life late after trailing 7-0.

Corey Seager drove in four runs in the final three innings with a homer and a double, while Mookie Betts, Max Muncy and Cody Bellinger each had his first hit of the series in a four-run ninth-inning rally that fell short.

"I thought that just late, us showing some life offensively was very good to see," manager Dave Roberts said. "To see us fighting, that was a good thing."

Kershaw was scratched because of back spasms not long before the left-hander was to make his second appearance — both in the playoffs the past week — a few miles from the three-time Cy Young Award winner's hometown of Dallas. Tony Gonsolin filled in, pitching three perfect innings in his postseason debut before allowing five runs while getting just four more outs.

For six innings, not even periodic chants of "Let's go, Dodgers" from the pandemic-reduced, mostly masked crowd of 10,624 could help in the second game with fans this season. The first was the series opener in the new 40,518-seat home of the Texas Rangers.

With the bases loaded and two outs in a scoreless game in the third, Smith bounced into a force out at third base. The Dodgers, who led the majors in runs during the regular season, didn't put more than one runner on base in an inning again until they trailed 7-0 in the seventh.

Then LA finally gave Dodgers fans a reason to get loud.

"I think all night we took better ABs," Seager said. "We go through the middle parts of the innings last night and kind of the ABs got away from us, had some quick innings. All tonight, we had really good ABs and just continue that tomorrow."

Seager's three-run homer in the seventh inning provided LA's first runs, and his double in the ninth drove home Betts, whose first hit of the series was a single.

Muncy's two-run homer pulled the Dodgers within two and forced Atlanta to use closer Mark Melancon. Bellinger's triple scored Will Smith before AJ Pollock hit a game-ending groundout to third.

"For us to be able to get Melancon in the game, in a game like this when we were down 7-0, I thought was big," Roberts said. "To see some other arms that we hadn't seen yet in the series I thought was important."

The NL's best bullpen faltered for the second straight night, this time early instead of late after the Dodgers gave up four runs in the ninth inning of a 5-1 loss in the opener. LA tied an LCS record by allowing four walks in an inning, two by Gonsolin and two from lefty reliever Pedro Báez in Atlanta's four-run fifth.

There was still no sign of Jansen, the cutter-throwing right-hander who was bypassed with the score tied in the ninth inning of the opener. The club's career leader in saves has been struggling with velocity and command, and he hasn't pitched since he couldn't finish LA's Game 2 win in the Division Series against San Diego.

Alex Wood gave up a run on two hits while walking two and hitting a batter in the left-hander's first postseason appearance since 2018, when he came out of the bullpen nine times. Lefty Adam Kolarek surrendered Ozzie Albies' second ninth-inning homer of the series.

"I think we did a good job of getting other guys in there to get their feet wet as far as in this series, to not stress them, for them to be available in the coming days," Roberts said of what will be the first NLCS without days off in 42 years. "You just can't play every game regardless of score like it's life or death in a seven-game series."

Despite the late rally, it's getting close to that for the Dodgers.

Facing: Cody Bellinger celebrates after a RBI triple against the Braves during the ninth inning.
AP PHOTO/
DAVID J. PHILLIP

Tony Gonsolin leaves Game 2 during the fifth inning.
AP PHOTO/ERIC GAY

Surging Back in the Series

Dodgers land
1st inning
haymaker to
knock out
Braves

October 14, 2020

ARLINGTON, TEXAS — The Los Angeles Dodgers and their predecessors from Brooklyn have been playing baseball for well over a century and have participated in dozens of playoff series across the country.

But in all that history, they never had a playoff game quite like Wednesday's, a bizarre contest that featured an unprecedented postseason offensive eruption in a neutral-site park in an American League city.

Just another quirky landmark in the oddest sports year yet.

The Dodgers summarily pounded the Atlanta Braves, 15-3, in Game 3 of the National League Championship Series at Globe Life Field, in a trouncing that established a catalog of records.

The Dodgers scored the most runs and hit the most home runs they ever had in a postseason game — and they accomplished all of that in just the first three innings.

"That was fun to be a part of," said Dodgers outfielder Joc Pederson, who hit a three-run home run to go with three other hits.

The Dodgers hit five home runs, including a grand slam by Max Muncy in a first inning that was so one-sided, it seemed surreal. Dodgers runners just kept circling the bases, until they had touched home plate 11 times — and, yes, that was a record, too — and it all happened before Atlanta's first turn at bat. It was the most runs scored in a single inning of a postseason game, according to the Elias Sports Bureau, besting the previous high by one run.

There were two walks, two singles, two doubles and three home runs in the inning, including back-to-back shots by Pederson and Edwin Rios before Muncy's slam. There was nothing Kyle Wright, the Braves' shellshocked starting pitcher, could do to stop the onslaught.

If there was a silver-ish lining for Atlanta, it was that they held the Dodgers scoreless over the final six innings without relying on their most important relief pitchers in a blowout. Atlanta also took several of its players out of the game, giving them a break that could prove critical in a seven-game series with no days off.

"The last four hours were not a lot of fun," Braves Manager Brian Snitker said after the game, "but as you look back, if you lose the game, that's probably the best possible way."

Many fans had traveled 800 miles from Atlanta to see their team play in the first baseball series with spectators this season, but many had checked out before the first inning was over — just like Wright.

Wright said he did not was in no rush to forget about the game, because then he would not learn from it.

"You can either feel sorry for yourself or find a way to bounce back," he said. "Learning from it and getting better is what I'm going to do."

The Dodgers matched the record set by the Braves in 1996 for most runs in an N.L.C.S. game. The high mark for runs in any league championship series game is 19, set by the Yankees in Game 3 of the 2004 A.L.C.S. at Boston, which gave the Yankees a 3-0 lead in that series (the Red Sox, of course, won the next four games).

The Dodgers' five homers matched the record for the most by any team in an L.C.S. game, and the 12-run margin of victory was the largest in the club's postseason history.

The Dodgers still trail the Braves by two games to one in the best-of-seven series, but momentum has been wrenched away from Atlanta by Los Angeles's perpetually dangerous offense.

That process actually may have begun in the late innings of Game 2, on Tuesday. In Game 1 of the series, the Braves limited the Dodgers to one run, then held them scoreless through the first six innings of Game 2. But the Dodgers have one of the most feared offenses in baseball, scoring the most runs in the regular season (349 — one more than the Braves).

In the ninth inning of Game 2, they scored four times before ultimately falling short in an 8-7 loss. But, after having trailed by 7-0 at one point, it was a signal that their slumping bats had awoken, and it carried into Game 3.

"I do think last night's ninth bled over into tonight," said Dave Roberts, the Dodgers' manager. "It was just a fun offensive night for us."

It seemed everything the Dodgers did set some kind of record: They had 18 total bases in the first inning, a league championship series record, and five extra-base hits, which tied the N.L.C.S. record.

The only record either team is really interested in, though, is becoming the first team to win an N.L.C.S. at an American League park, and earning a spot in the World Series.

Facing: Edwin Rios celebrates his home run during the first inning of Game 3.
AP PHOTO/ERIC GAY

Max Muncy celebrates his grand slam during the first inning in Game 3.
AP PHOTO/TONY GUTIERREZ

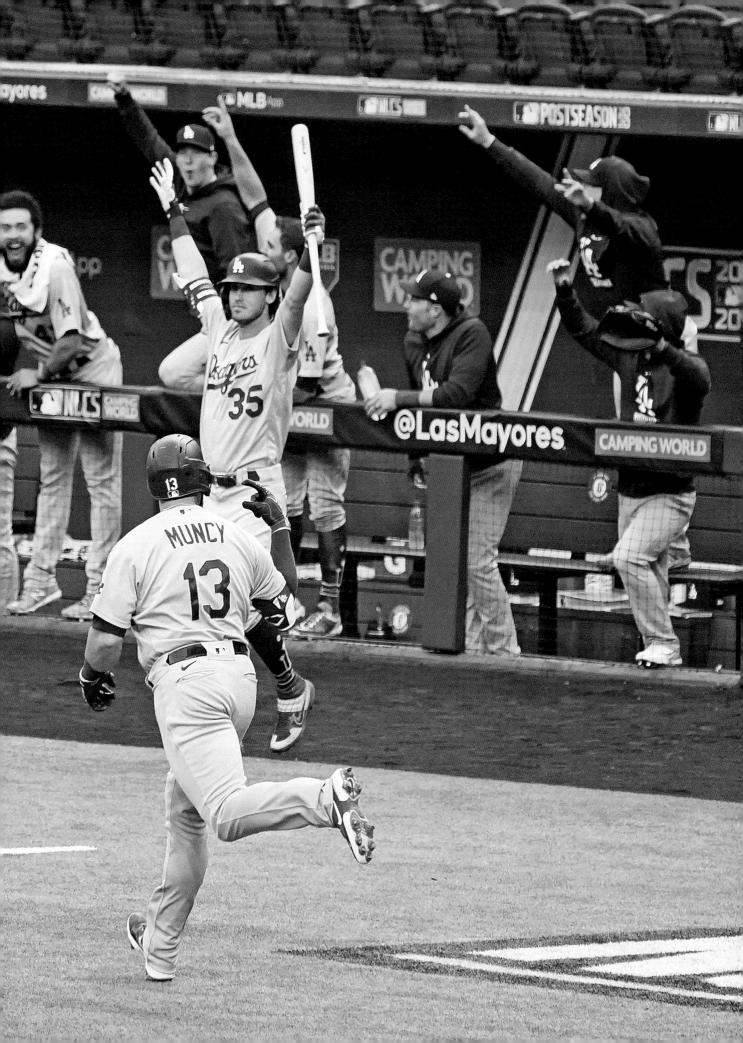

No Answer, and in Trouble

Dodgers
pushed to
brink of
elimination

October 16, 2020

ARLINGTON, TEXAS — Clayton Kershaw made the slow trudge to that lonely spot in the dugout once again, this time just a few miles from his hometown.

The longtime ace of the Dodgers just can't shake his playoff curse, not even on friendly turf in a neutral-site NL Championship Series.

Kershaw faltered at the start of the sixth inning against Atlanta, allowing three straight hits before watching the rest of a six-run outburst in the Braves' 10-2 win in Game 4 on Thursday night.

Kershaw's franchise-high 12th postseason loss put Los Angeles down 3-1 in the best-of-seven series at the home of the Texas Rangers, on the brink of a second straight defeat in the NLCS after posting the best record in the majors during the pandemic-shortened season.

Pitching two days after he was scratched from a Game 2 start because of back spasms, Kershaw allowed four runs in five-plus innings, boosting his career playoff ERA to 4.31.

While the three-time NL Cy Young Award winner is also the club's career leader in postseason wins with his 11-12 record, his October resume simply doesn't match his stellar regular-season numbers: 175-76 with a 2.43 ERA.

In LA's seven trips to the NLCS over Kershaw's 13 seasons, the Dallas native is 3-6 with a 4.84 ERA. And now the left-hander has been outpitched by a rookie making his postseason debut: Atlanta's 22-year-old Game 4 winner, Bryse Wilson.

"I think that he came out and five innings, one run, again, what happened right there in that sixth inning, he gave us a chance to win the baseball game," manager Dave Roberts said. "We couldn't put any runs up early and get a lead, or hold a lead. That narrative couldn't be further from the truth."

Kershaw was handed a 1-0 lead on Edwin Ríos' homer in the third, but gave it up on Marcell Ozuna's solo shot in the fourth, the first of two for Ozuna.

In the sixth, Ronald Acuña Jr.'s high chopper eluded the glove of a leaping Kershaw behind the mound for an infield single. Freddie Freeman and Ozuna followed with consecutive RBI doubles, and Kershaw was done in Los Angeles' third loss in four games since winning its first five in the playoffs.

"It would have been nice to get Acuna out," Kershaw said. "Just part of playing on turf. He kind of chopped that one up. Freddie, I had two strikes on him. Probably just went one too many pitches inside."

Kershaw had never pitched near his Dallas home before doing so twice in a week and a half in this unusual postseason, first without fans in an NL Division Series sweep of San Diego and then a pandemic-reduced crowd in the NLCS.

The eight-time All-Star recorded his 11th postseason win in the Dodgers' 6-5 victory in Game 2 of the NLDS, but he was far from dominant. Manny Machado and Eric Hosmer hit back-to-back homers to cut into a 4-1 deficit.

A night after becoming the first team to score 11 runs in an inning and the first with 15 runs and five homers in the first three innings of a postseason game, the Dodgers had just three hits. Ríos' homer was their only hit before Kershaw exited.

"Every time Kershaw gets on that mound, you want to score 20," Ríos said. "You want to score as many runs as we can for him. It was unfortunate we weren't able to do that tonight."

If the Hall of Fame is in his future, Kershaw won't be alone among star pitchers who struggled in the playoffs.

Greg Maddux was 11-14 in the postseason, most of those decisions when Atlanta won just one World Series during a run of 14 straight NL East titles. Randy Johnson was 7-9, and fellow lefty Steve Carlton just 6-6.

Another lefty, David Price, was 2-9 before winning his final three decisions for Boston when the Red Sox won the World Series two years ago.

Each of those pitchers has at least one title, though. Kershaw still doesn't have one despite the club record in playoff starts (28) and innings (177 1/3).

Kershaw now has 11 career postseason starts of allowing at least four runs, tied with Maddux for the second-most. Only Andy Pettitte, another lefty, has more.

Ozuna's first homer in Game 4 was the 27th Kershaw has allowed in the playoffs, breaking a tie with Justin Verlander for second-most, also behind Pettitte (31).

Clayton Kershaw
watches as the
Atlanta Braves take
the lead in the sixth
inning in Game 4.
KYODO

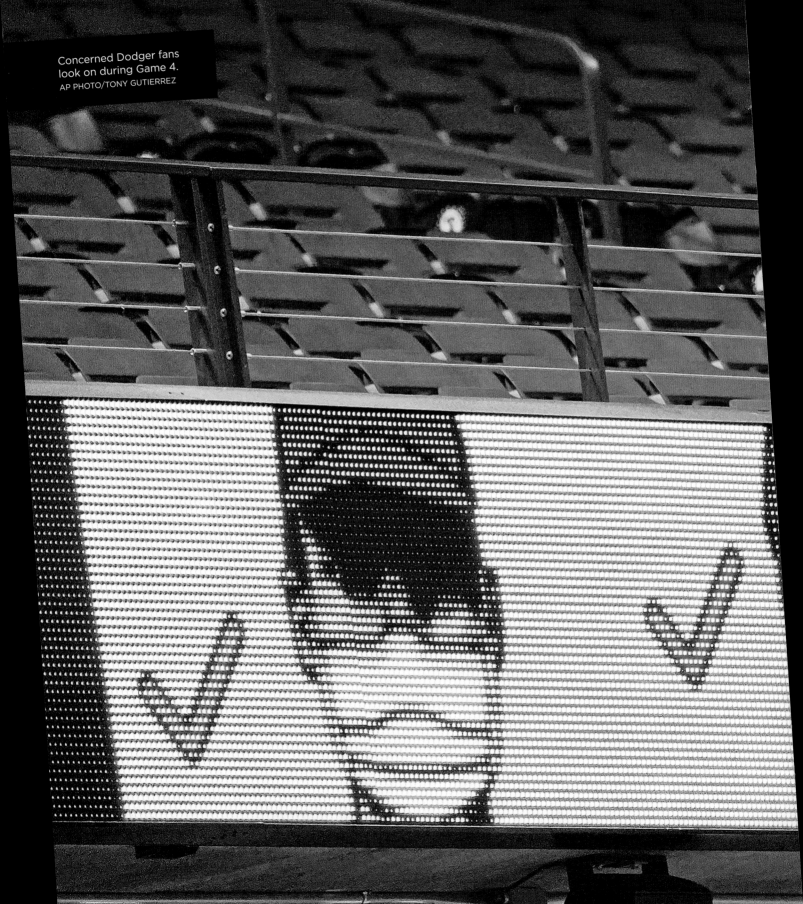

Stayin' Alive

Smith, Seager
lead Dodgers
past Braves in
Game 5

October 17, 2020

ARLINGTON, TEXAS — One Will Smith outdid another Will Smith to keep the season alive for the Los Angeles Dodgers.

A common name, a special result for the Dodgers catcher.

Smith hit a go-ahead, three-run homer off the Atlanta Braves reliever with the same name, Corey Seager homered twice and the Dodgers avoided elimination with a 7-3 win in Game 5 of the NL Championship Series on Friday night.

"I'll always bet on our Will Smith," Dodges manager Dave Roberts said.

Smith connected in the sixth against — of all people — Will Smith, the fourth of six Braves pitchers in their bullpen night that started with a couple of postseason firsts by A.J. Minter.

"For him to come through for us in that spot. I'm happy to see him expressing himself," Dodgers right fielder Mookie Betts said of his teammate who rarely shows emotion but was clearly pumped up by his big blast.

Betts got that decisive sixth started with an infield single, and the first-year Dodger and former AL MVP had a running, shoestring catch in right field that turned into an inning-ending double play. His snag took an Atlanta run off the board after a replay challenge right before Seager's first homer.

"You're talking about momentum shifts, that's the play of the year," Roberts said. "I just thought there was no way he was going to make that play."

Game 6 is Saturday afternoon, with a pitching rematch from the series opener: lefty Max Fried for the Braves and right-hander Walker Buehler for the Dodgers. Both gave up one run in Game 1, which Atlanta won 5-1 after a four-run ninth. Atlanta is looking to get into the World Series for the first time since 1999.

"I knew it was going to be a really hard series, regardless of what situation you're in," Braves manager Brian Snitker said. "I feel good tomorrow with Max on the mound. I feel really good with him going out there. Hopefully we can score a few runs and support him and wrap this thing up."

Betts had a stolen base after his sixth-starting single before Justin Turner's one-out hard grounder that got Betts caught in a rundown. The Braves then brought in their lefty named Will Smith to face left-handed batter Max Muncy, who drew a walk before the Dodgers' catcher named Will Smith hit a full-count pitch 404 feet to left-center for a 4-2 lead.

"It got the team going. That energy bounces off of each other," Smith said.

It was the first time since at least 1961 that a batter homered off a pitcher with the same name in the regular season or postseason, according to the Elias Sports Bureau.

The Dodgers extended their lead in the seventh when Chris Taylor hit a two-out double and scored on a single by Betts before Seager hit a ball into LA's bullpen in right-center.

Seager's four homers and 10 RBIs have already tied NLCS records, with at least one more game for the Dodgers to play — two if they want a chance to get to the World Series for the third time in four years. The four homers are already a record for a shortstop in any postseason series.

"Just kind of putting good swings on pitches and everything is kind of clicking," Seager said.

After Marcell Ozuna and Travis d'Arnaud had consecutive singles to start the third for Atlanta, there was one out when Dansby Swanson hit a sinking liner to right. Betts made a running catch, with his glove skimming the ground before his throw home was late. But the Dodgers challenged that Ozuna that left third base early — and it became the Braves third out instead of their third run.

"We were able to get a stop," Betts said. "Yesterday we couldn't stop the bleeding. Today, we were able to get a stop right there and put some pressure on them."

Umpires and the off-site replay crew needed nearly two minutes to make their ruling, but Dodgers fielders — and even Braves runners — had already left the field after watching the play on the big video board.

"It's not always on the offensive side that you get the spark," Seager said. "A big play in a big moment you get some energy."

Right after that, Seager's leadoff homer to straightaway center in the fourth cut the Dodgers deficit to 2-1.

Rookie center fielder Cristian Pache made a leaping try at the wall, but the ball went just behind his extended glove. But Pache did time things up in the eighth, robbing Muncy of a homer with a nearly identical play.

The Braves scored in both innings off LA starter Dustin May. Freddie Freeman doubled, went to third and scored on d'Arnaud's sacrifice fly in the first, and Pache had an RBI single in the second. D'Arnaud added an RBI groundout in the eighth.

Facing: Will Smith
watches his three-run
home run in the sixth
inning of Game 5.
AP PHOTO/SUE OGROCKI

The Dodgers celebrate a three-run home run by Will Smith in Game 5.

Seager Swings for Season

October 18, 2020

Dodger stays hot, homers again in 3-1 win as L.A. forces Game 7

ARLINGTON, TEXAS — Corey Seager's sweet swing. Walker Buehler's calm. Kenley Jansen's resurgence.

The Los Angeles Dodgers got what they needed — again.

"We did what we had to do to force a Game 7," Justin Turner said.

They sure did.

Seager homered again, Buehler pitched six scoreless innings and the Dodgers beat the Atlanta Braves 3-1 on Saturday to send the NL Championship Series to a winner-take-all finale.

Los Angeles avoided elimination for the second time in less than 24 hours, staying alive in its pursuit of a third pennant in four years. It hasn't won a championship since 1988.

"I'm still sort of recovering from this one, but already thinking about Game 7," Dodgers manager Dave Roberts said. "That's what you live for."

Turner also homered for Los Angeles, and Jansen threw a six-pitch ninth for his 18th career postseason save.

Roberts was keeping his options open for his Game 7 starting pitcher while the Braves plan to go with rookie right-hander Ian Anderson, who has thrown 15 2/3 scoreless innings in his three postseason starts. Tony Gonsolin and three-time NL Cy Young Award winner Clayton Kershaw are among the possibilities for Los Angeles.

"Shoot, we'll go out there and let 'er fly. A Game 7 is another baseball game," Atlanta manager Brian Snitker said. "You have to treat it as such."

The Braves were hoping to celebrate Snitker's 65th birthday Saturday with the franchise's first World Series berth since 1999. But Max Fried took his first loss all year, working into the seventh inning after surrendering three runs during a rocky first.

Buehler, using Stan's Rodeo Ointment to deal with bothersome blisters, threw 65 of his 89 pitches for strikes. He allowed seven hits while striking out six without a walk.

After Atlanta loaded the bases with three singles in a row to start the top of second — the last hit by his Vanderbilt roommate Dansby Swanson — the right-hander really brought the heat, with 10 consecutive fastballs to get out of the jam.

Buehler said he has never felt that calm in a game, especially a situation like that. He credited catcher Austin Barnes — and past experiences.

"I've failed in those moments. I've been through it and I've been good after it, but that failure doesn't really scare me anymore," Buehler said. "The more times you go through things like that, your heartbeat kind of changes and can slow down."

Fried, who struck out five and walked four in 6 2/3 innings, allowed only two homers in his 11 starts while going 7-0 during the regular season. But the Dodgers went deep twice in three pitches in the first.

Seager pulled a towering shot to right on a 73-mph curveball, and Turner connected on a 93-mph sinker that went 418 feet to straightaway center. Max Muncy walked and scored after back-to-back singles by Will Smith and Cody Bellinger that made it 3-0.

"I came out in a game like this and kind of put us behind the eight-ball real quick." Fried said. "To me, that's unacceptable."

Seager, who homered twice in Game 5 on Friday night, has NLCS records with five homers and 11 RBIs, and still a game to play. His six homers overall are already a Dodgers postseason record.

Mookie Betts, the 2018 AL MVP and first-year Dodger, made a leaping catch against the right field wall to end the fifth. While it wouldn't have been a homer, it robbed Marcell Ozuna of extra bases, and the Braves a likely run.

Betts let out an emphatic shout while pumping both fists, then celebrated with Bellinger while Buehler held his right arm high in the air.

With Buehler out of the game, Nick Markakis greeted Blake Treinen with triple to right leading off off the seventh and came home on a one-out double by Ronald Acuña Jr.

But the Dodgers' bullpen closed it out from there, with Jansen finishing the victory in an encouraging performance heading into Game 7.

It was Jansen's first save chance in five appearances since closing out the Dodgers' first playoff win this season in the wild-card round. He struck out the side on 12 pitches in Friday night's 7-3 win.

"Two huge outings, not only for us, but him personally, you can just see the confidence he has on the mound attacking guys," Turner said. "That's the Kenley Jansen I and all of us in there all know and love."

Facing: Mookie Betts robs Atlanta Braves' Marcell Ozuna of a home run during the fifth inning in Game 6.
AP PHOTO/TONY GUTIERREZ

Corey Seager delivers a first-inning home run in Game 6.
AP PHOTO/SUE OGROCKI

Back to the Show!

Bellinger's home run sends Dodgers to third World Series in four years

October 19, 2020

ARLINGTON, TEXAS — The Los Angeles Dodgers celebrated as Cody Bellinger's drive soared deep into the Texas night. Bellinger flung his bat off to the side and strutted up the first-base line.

All the way to the World Series.

Bellinger hit a tiebreaking solo homer in the seventh inning, and the Dodgers advanced to the Fall Classic for the third time in four years by topping the Atlanta Braves 4-3 in Game 7 of the NL Championship Series on Sunday.

"This year is our year," manager Dave Roberts said.

Bellinger connected an inning after Kiké Hernández became the first pinch hitter with a game-tying or go-ahead homer in a winner-take-all-game. His homer tied it at 3 and, like Bellinger's, came on the eighth pitch of the at-bat.

The Dodgers, who matched an LCS record with 16 homers, overcame a 3-1 series deficit by winning three consecutive games when facing elimination for only the second time in their storied history.

"Defensively, pitching, game-calling, planning, everything. we grinded all the way through this series," said shortstop Corey Seager, who was named NLCS MVP after bashing a record five homers in the series. "We're glad to be on top."

Julio Urias closed with three perfect innings as the Dodgers won their 24th NL pennant, their 12th since moving to Los Angeles. They are coming off their eighth consecutive NL West title.

The Dodgers are once again going for their first World Series title since 1988. They lost Game 7 at home three years ago to to the Houston Astros, and then lost in five games to the Boston Red Sox in 2018 when Mookie Betts was the AL MVP and playing against Los Angeles.

Tampa Bay's win in Game 7 of the ALCS late Saturday night wiped out the chance for an October rematch with the Astros, whose 2017 World Series victory over the Dodgers has been heavily tarnished by the revelations of Houston's sign-stealing tactics that season.

Betts, the first-year Dodger signed for 12 more years, made another incredible defensive play, robbing Freeman of a solo homer in the fifth. He had run-saving plays in all three of their potential elimination games.

"This is really the first time we've had our backs against the wall," Betts said. "It seemed like we were getting handled a little bit early on. We were able to get a hold of ourselves and fight back. We're never going to give up."

Urias, the fifth Dodgers pitcher, got his fourth win in four appearances this postseason. The 24-year-old right-hander, already in his fourth postseason, has a 0.57 ERA in these playoffs.

"That's his moment right there. That was his game to win and he went out there and did it," Seager said.

The massive shot to right by reigning NL MVP and 2018 NLCS MVP Bellinger came on a 94-mph sinker after fouling off three pitches in a row by Chris Martin, the fifth Braves pitcher who started the seventh with strikeouts of Max Muncy and Will Smith.

Hernández led off the sixth with a 424-foot drive to left-center off A.J. Minter.

"Game 7 of the NLCS, win or go home, I was ready from first pitch of the game on. Mentally prepared, physically ready, envisioning AB situations," Hernández said.

Dansby Swanson homered for Atlanta, which hasn't been to the World Series since 1999.

Before the late drama, it was the first winner-take-all game in postseason history matching rookie starters.

The Dodgers scored twice in the third to tie it at 2, the first runs allowed by Ian Anderson in his four postseason starts — the 22-year-old right-hander started only six games for Atlanta in the regular season. His scoreless streak of 17 2/3 innings was the third-longest to start a postseason career.

Justin Turner drew a two-out walk, Muncy doubled and Will Smith bounced a two-run single through the open gap near second created by the defensive shift.

The Dodgers' Dustin May became the first pitcher to walk the first two batters in a winner-take-all-game — and the 23-year-old from nearby Justin, Texas, did so without throwing a strike to Ronald Acuna Jr. or Freeman. The Braves didn't even swing at a pitch until Marcell Ozuna's sharp single through the left side of the infield on an 0-1 curveball for a 1-0 lead.

"We believed we should have been in the World Series," Freeman said. "It's just the Dodgers came, and they won three games in a row. I feel like you can hang your head high. We gave it everything we had."

Facing: Cody Bellinger celebrates his seventh inning home run with A.J. Pollock.

AP PHOTO/ERIC GAY

Julio Urias celebrates the Dodgers win against the Atlanta Braves in Game 7.
AP PHOTO/TONY GUTIERREZ

Promising Start

Kershaw, Bellinger, Betts lead way for Dodgers in Game 1

October 20, 2020

ARLINGTON, TEXAS — Clayton Kershaw, Cody Bellinger, Mookie Betts and the Los Angeles Dodgers left the Tampa Bay Rays stuck in neutral to start a most strange World Series played amid the pandemic.

Kershaw dominated for six innings, Bellinger and Betts homered and the Dodgers chased a wild Tyler Glasnow in the fifth inning for an 8-3 win in Game 1 of the first Series held at a neutral site.

A crowd limited by the coronavirus to 11,388 at Globe Life Field, the new $1.2 billion home of the Texas Rangers, marked the smallest for baseball's top event in 111 years.

"It's hard not to think about winning. It's hard not to think about what that might be like," Kershaw said. "Constantly keep putting that in your brain: tomorrow, win tomorrow, win tomorrow, win tomorrow. You do that three more times, and you can think about it all you want."

A regular season star with an erratic postseason history, Kershaw looked like the ace who so often stars on midsummer evenings with the San Gabriel Mountains behind him at Dodger Stadium. With these games shifted, the 32-year-old left-hander wound up pitching not far from his offseason home in Dallas.

The three-time Cy Young Award winner allowed one run and two hits, struck out eight and walked one. He induced 19 swings and misses among his 78 pitches — more than his three previous Series starts combined.

"You can appreciate and totally see why he's heading to the Hall of Fame one day whenever he's done," Rays manager Kevin Cash said.

Kershaw threw nine balls in the first, when he stranded a pair of runners, then threw just nine more over the next three innings.

"He had a game plan to try to really quiet down things from there and he executed," said Kevin Kiermeier, who ended Kershaw's streak of 13 retired in a row with a fifth-inning homer that cut the Rays' deficit to 2-1.

Kershaw, a five-time ERA champ, improved to 2-2 in the World Series and 12-12 in postseason play, a shadow of his 175-76 regular season record.

Bellinger, the 2019 NL MVP who began the opener with a career .114 batting average in 12 World Series games, had put the Dodgers ahead in the fourth with a two-run homer off Glasnow, having no trouble driving a 98 mph pitch into the Dodgers bullpen in right-center.

Bellinger, whose seventh-inning homer put the Dodgers ahead in Game 7 of the NL Championship, raised an arm triumphantly while Glasnow turned and watched the ball sail out.

He shuffled his feet, tapping gently as he crossed the plate and celebrated while dancing back to the dugout, a sign he remembered popping his right shoulder during raucous revelry two nights earlier. Bellinger capped his evening by leaping at the 6-foot center field wall in the ninth, robbing Austin Meadows of a possible home run.

"I said it today before the game: If I hit one I'm not touching anybody's arm," Bellinger said. "I'm going straight foot, and it was pretty funny."

Betts, brilliant throughout October but slumping at the plate, added his first postseason homer for the Dodgers, a solo shot in the sixth off Josh Fleming.

Betts had two hits, scored two runs and stole two bases in the four-run fifth, when Corey Seager swiped one as Los Angeles became the first team to steal three bases in a Series inning since the 1912 New York Giants in Game 5 against Boston.

"Stolen bases are a thing for me. That's how I create runs and create havoc on the basepaths," he said.

After helping Boston beat the Dodgers in the 2018 Series, Betts was traded to LA before this season. The former AL MVP showed off his defensive skills in the NLCS with three terrific catches.

Los Angeles is in the Series for the third time in four years but seeking its first title since the Kirk Gibson- and Orel Hershiser-led team of 1988. Coming off an unusual LCS of games on seven straight days, the Dodgers planned an all-bullpen outing for the next game.

Tampa Bay's only previous Series was a five-game loss to Philadelphia in 2008.

An overwhelming majority of the 10,535 fans in attendance wore Dodger blue.

"They're everywhere. They always come out," Kershaw said. "And so as much as we would have liked it to have been at Dodger Stadium with 56,000 chanting fans, after everything that's gone on this season, to have a 10-, 11,000 people in the stands and the majority be big Dodger fans, this is pretty cool and definitely helps us for sure."

Facing: Cody Bellinger makes a leaping catch to rob Austin Meadows of a home run in the ninth inning in Game 1.
KYODO VIA AP IMAGES

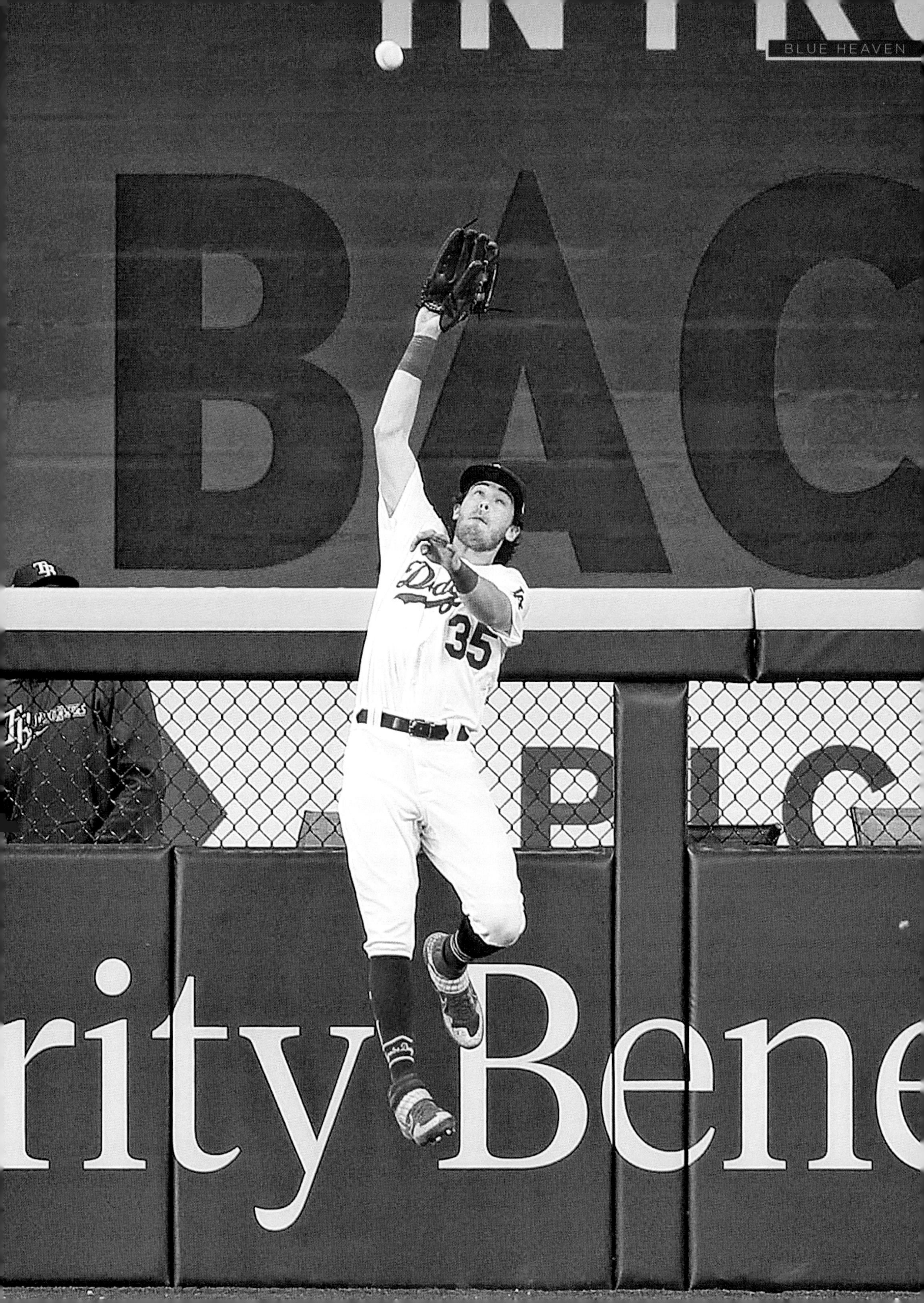
BAC
35
rity Bene

Mookie Betts scores past Rays catcher Mike Zunino on a fielders choice by Max Muncy.

AP PHOTO/DAVID J. PHILLIP

Lowe's Homers Even it Up

Joey Wendle adds three RBI in 6-4 Tampa Bay win

October 21, 2020

ARLINGTON, TEXAS — Brandon Lowe busted out early and Tampa Bay's bullpen hung on late. Rays and Dodgers, tied in Texas.

Lowe shook loose from his extended postseason slump with two opposite-field home runs, and Tampa Bay held off Los Angeles 6-4 to square the World Series at one game apiece.

"Yeah, those felt really good," said Lowe, a 2019 All-Star who led the Rays with 14 homers and 37 RBIs this season. "It felt great to kind of get back and contribute to the team. You know, they've been doing so well for the past month — it felt really good to get back and actually start doing stuff again."

Blake Snell struck out nine in 4 2/3 innings for the Rays and didn't allow a hit until Chris Taylor's two-run homer trimmed it to 5-2 in the fifth. The Dodgers threatened to complete a big comeback in the eighth, but Tampa Bay's relievers held firm.

Lowe and Joey Wendle each drove in three runs for the Rays.

Nick Anderson got four outs for the win. Diego Castillo earned the save when he struck out Taylor, the only batter he faced.

Left-hander Aaron Loup also did a nice job, throwing a called third strike past Cody Bellinger with a runner on second to end the eighth before retiring the first two hitters in the ninth.

After an off day, Game 3 in the best-of-seven Series matches two big-game pitchers starting on extra rest Friday night. Charlie Morton gets the ball for Tampa Bay against Walker Buehler.

Lowe hit an opposite-field solo homer to left-center in the first off Tony Gonsolin, putting the American League champion Rays ahead for the first time at this neutral-site World Series with their 27th home run of the postseason, matching a major league record. The second baseman was hitting .107 this postseason, and in an even worse 4-for-48 slide (.083) the past 13 games since the start of the AL Division Series.

"Sometimes guys, you've got to allow them to go through some tough patches, and he's been in one," Rays manager Kevin Cash said. "He will go quiet for a little while, but he can get as hot as anybody in baseball."

By the time he went deep again in the fifth, his second opposite-field shot of the game and the entire season — with a runner on against Dustin May, already the fourth Dodgers pitcher — it was 5-0.

Will Smith and NLCS MVP Corey Seager also homered for the Dodgers. Seager's solo shot in the eighth was his seventh homer and 16th RBI, extended the franchise records he had already set this postseason. Those are also the most homers by a shortstop in any MLB postseason.

Snell already had all his strikeouts when he walked Kiké Hernández with two outs in the fifth before Taylor, the No. 9 batter, homered on his 80th pitch. The Rays ace was out of the game two batters later, after Mookie Betts walked and Seager singled.

"He was outstanding," Cash said. "The slider from my vantage looked like it was a really good weapon for him. He was awesome. Gave us everything that we needed."

Anderson got out of the jam with a strikeout of Justin Turner.

The Dodgers knew it would be primarily a bullpen game using various arms, instead of bringing back Buehler on short rest after ace lefty Clayton Kershaw threw six strong innings in their 8-3 win in Game 1.

Four of the first five LA pitchers allowed runs, with Dylan Floro keeping a clean slate after benefiting from a nice defensive play and a replay review that ended the second. Gonsolin, the rookie right-hander who started, allowed Lowe's first homer and was done after 1 1/3 innings.

Snell threw only 10 pitches in a 1-2-3 first that included strikeouts of Betts and Turner. After 11 of his first 15 pitches in the second inning were balls, among two walks and a strikeout, the 2018 Al Cy Young Award winner retired the next 10 batters until the walk to Hernández in the fifth.

The left-hander was attacking with breaking pitches in the strike zone, not his usual pattern, since the Dodgers don't often chase. But Los Angeles didn't get many bats on the ball against him. Smith homered for Los Angeles in the sixth off Anderson.

A bobble by Hernández at second base proved costly, taking away a potential inning-ending double play in the fourth before the Dodgers changed pitchers again and gave up two runs.

With one out and Randy Arozarena at first, Ji-Man Choi hit a grounder to Hernández, and by time the second baseman gathered the ball to get the force, Seager's relay throw was late. Manuel Margot then greeted May, the third reliever, with a single before Wendle's two-run double into the right-center gap for a 3-0 lead.

Wendle added a sacrifice fly in the sixth.

Willy Adames
and Brandon Lowe
celebrate their win
in Game 2.
AP PHOTO/ERIC GAY

Chris Taylor hits a two-run home run during the fifth inning in Game 2.
AP PHOTO/SUE OGROCKI

Buehler Stymies Rays

Turner and
Barnes both
hit homers in
6-2 Dodgers
win

October 23, 2020

ARLINGTON, TEXAS — Walker Buehler was dominant for Los Angeles. Just like Orel Hershiser during the Dodgers' last title run.

Buehler struck out 10 in six innings in a pulsating performance, and Los Angeles beat the Tampa Bay Rays 6-2 for a 2-1 World Series lead.

"He was unbelievable. He really was," said Dodgers catcher Austin Barnes, who himself made history by homering and driving in a run via sacrifice bunt, the first player to do both in the same World Series game in nearly 60 years. "He made it really easy on me. That might have been the best I've ever seen his stuff really."

Justin Turner homered in the first inning against a surprisingly hittable Charlie Morton, who was chased in the fifth.

Los Angeles overwhelmed Tampa Bay in all phases, leaving the Rays' scuffling offense with a .206 average and 11 runs in the Series.

Thirty-eight of 59 previous teams that won Game 3 for a 2-1 lead went on to take the title.

Steely-eyed like the Hershiser who won MVP honors of the 1988 Series, Buehler has supplanted Clayton Kershaw as the Dodgers' ace. He allowed three of Tampa Bay's four hits and walked one.

The 26-year-old right-hander has allowed one run in 13 Series innings that include seven scoreless in Game 3 against Boston two years ago. He improved to 2-0 with a 1.80 ERA in four postseason starts that include the win over Atlanta in Game 6 of the NL Championship Series last weekend.

He started 15 of 21 batters with strikes and threw strikes on 67 of 93 pitches. Buehler didn't allow a hit until Manuel Margot's one-out double in the fifth. Willy Adames then drove in Margot with another double.

The Rays' only other hit off him was Austin Meadows' leadoff single in the sixth.

"I haven't put it all together and grasped or wrapped my head around all that he's accomplished in this short period of time," Dodgers manager Dave Roberts said of Buehler. "Being a big-game pitcher and really succeeding on this stage, there's only a few guys currently and throughout history. He's in some really elite company, and I'm just happy he's wearing a Dodger uniform."

Tampa Bay batters were kept off balance by his mix of 59 four-seam fastballs, 14 knuckle-curves, 12 sliders and eight cut fastballs. He became the first pitcher in the Series with 10 or more strikeouts in six or fewer innings, part of analytic changes in modern baseball that have led to shorter starter outings in an era of vastly increased whiffs.

Buehler cruised in his final inning, striking out Mike Zunino, Brandon Lowe and Randy Arozarena swinging to reach double digits -- the first 10-strikeout game of his postseason career.

"The fastball command was incredible," Turner said. "And just the way he pitches and attacks and how aggressive he is going right at guys. He'll mix in a cutter or a slider, or a curveball to lefties. But he pitches with his fastball. And he's aggressive with it. And it is what it is. You know he's going to throw it, and he says hit it if you can, and he got a lot of swings and misses tonight."

Blake Treinen and Brusdar Graterol followed with a scoreless inning apiece. Kenley Jansen gave up Randy Arozarena's eighth homer of the postseason in the ninth before closing it out.

Morton, a right-hander who turns 37 on Nov. 12, had entered unbeaten in seven straight postseason decisions, one shy of Orlando Hernandez's record, including wins in five consecutive postseason starts. But he took the loss, allowing five runs and seven hits in 4 1/3 innings — more than the four runs total he gave up in his previous five postseason starts combined.

No Rays starter has finished the fifth inning in their last five Series starts since Matt Garza in Game 3 against Philadelphia in 2008. Tampa Bay repeated its pattern of a dozen years ago, losing the opener, winning the next game and dropping the third,

Turner put the Dodgers ahead on Morton's 14th pitch, turning on a high 94.8 mph fastball with a 1-2 count and driving the ball 397 feet over the left-field wall. Turner's home run was the Dodgers' team record 24th this postseason and the 11th of Turner's postseason career over 69 games, tying the team record set by Duke Snider over 36 games with the Brooklyn and Los Angeles Dodgers from 1954 to 1959.

Los Angeles extended the lead to 3-0 in the third when Morton hit Seager on a toe with a pitch, Turner doubled and Max Muncy drove a cutter into center for a two-run single.

After singles by Cody Bellinger and Joc Pederson, Barnes drove in a run with the safety squeeze to first baseman Ji-Man Choi, the first RBI bunt in the Series since the Rays' Jason Barlett in Game 2 in 2008 and the first since for the Dodgers since Billy Cox in Game 3 of 1953.

Facing: Walker
Buehler pitches in
Game 3.
KYODO VIA AP IMAGES

Justin Turner hits a home run during the first inning in Game 3.
AP PHOTO/SUE OGROCKI

Stumbling to a Tie

Rays stun Dodgers in epic Game 4 finish

October 24, 2020

ARLINGTON, TEXAS — Brett Phillips squatted on the field crying, Randy Arozarena sprawled in the dirt pounding his hands on home plate.

Tears of joy, smacks of celebration — and a crucial, crazy win for the scrappy Tampa Bay Rays.

In one of the wildest World Series finishes ever, the light-hitting Phillips delivered a tying single off Kenley Jansen with two outs in the bottom of the ninth inning that turned into the game-ending hit when the Los Angeles Dodgers dropped the ball twice, allowing Arozarena to scramble home and lifting the Rays to an 8-7 victory Saturday night that suddenly evened things at two games each.

"Golly, what a special moment," Phillips said.

The Dodgers led 7-6 when center fielder Chris Taylor misplayed Phillips' ball in right-center for an error and chased it down while Kevin Kiermaier scored the tying run. Arozarena kept charging around third base but stumbled and fell well before reaching home.

He was able to get up and score when catcher Will Smith looked up too early and missed the relay throw, letting it squirt toward the backstop while Arozarena dived on top of the plate.

"Once I saw Randy slip, I was like 'Aw, shoot, at least we tied it up,' and then he missed the ball," said Phillips, who had entered the game as a pinch-runner in the eighth. "I don't know what happened, but then he scored. The next thing I know, I'm airplane-ing around the outfield and I get dogpiled and here I am."

Arozarena said he was trying to retreat to third after tumbling over.

"We had already tied the game. I was trying to get into a rundown," Arozarena said through a translator. "Then obviously once the ball got past him, I turned around and scored."

A 26-year-old from Seminole, Florida, Phillips was drafted by Houston and played for Milwaukee and Kansas City before being acquired by the Rays, his hometown team, in August for a minor leaguer. Touted for his outfield defense and speed, he hasn't hit much in the majors, ending the regular season with a career .202 average in 153 games.

He had been 0 for 2 in the postseason and hadn't batted since Game 3 of the AL Division Series on Oct. 7. His last hit had been a month ago, on Sept. 25.

Phillips was left off the AL Championship Series roster but shined as a cheerleader, writing up phony scouting reports on a clipboard touting Arozarena before dancing against him in battles after the team locked up the AL pennant.

"What a great team effort on this win. It took almost 28 guys," Phillips said. "That's what special about this team. Just all come together, our one goal is to win. We don't rely on one guy. It takes everyone, and man, baseball is fun."

Corey Seager and Justin Turner both had four hits with a solo homer for the Dodgers, who nearly went into Game 5 with a 3-1 series lead.

Cody Bellinger, a Gold Glove finalist in center field, was switched to designated hitter just over an hour before the game because of back stiffness, trading places with AJ Pollock in the lineup. Taylor, also a second baseman, started in left field and moved to center after Joc Pederson pinch-hit for Pollock in the seventh and then took over in left. Only Taylor was charged with an error on the final play.

Turner said there was no way for Dodgers catcher Smith to have known Arozarena fell.

"He was trying to catch the ball and put a quick tag down. If he'd have known he fell, he probably would have taken his time and made sure he caught it," Turner said. "Not sure what happened in center. That's uncharacteristic for us."

Hunter Renfroe, Brandon Lowe and Kiermaier also homered for the Rays, who had gotten all of their runs on long balls until that last play. Those homers came during a frantic stretch when the teams combined to score in eight consecutive half-innings, a first in World Series history.

A solo homer by Kiermaier tied the game at 6 in the seventh, right after the first two lead changes in this entire World Series.

Lowe went deep the opposite way for the third time in this Series, his three-run homer to left in the bottom of the sixth putting the Rays up 5-4. A half-inning later, the second baseman was laying facedown in short right field after his diving attempt to catch Pederson's liner, which skimmed off the top of his glove for a two-run single that put LA back ahead.

That was the first go-ahead pinch-hit in the World Series for LA since Kirk Gibson's game-ending homer in Game 1 in 1988.

Dodgers pitcher
Brusdar Graterol
celebrates the last
out against the Rays
in the eighth inning in
Game 4.
AP PHOTO/
TONY GUTIERREZ

Randy Arozarena slides in to home to score in the bottom of the 9th inning, winning Game 4 and leveling the Series, 2-2.

AP PHOTO/DAVID J. PHILLIP

Ace's Sweet Redemption

Kershaw
pitches
Dodgers to
3-2 World
Series lead,
brink of title

October 25, 2020

ARLINGTON, TEXAS — As much as Clayton Kershaw has dominated hitters throughout a glittering career, he has not silenced those who cite his lack of baseball's ultimate accomplishment.

With a gritty performance, plus one particular delivery home that will long be remembered, he hushed the skeptics and moved the Los Angeles Dodgers within a victory of their first World Series title since 1988.

"He's a phenomenal pitcher on the biggest stage," reliever Blake Treinen said after Kershaw beat the Tampa Bay Rays for the second time in six days, a 4-2 win Sunday night that gave the Dodgers a 3-2 Series lead. "I think a lot of credit goes to what he's been able to do in this World Series for us."

Los Angeles was clinging to a one-run lead with runners at the corners and two outs in the fourth inning, and Kevin Kiermaier at the plate.

The great left-hander had raised both hands over his head in his instantly recognizable stretch position when he heard first baseman Max Muncy scream: "Step off! Step off! Step off!"

"Instinctually, I kind of did it," Kershaw recalled.

He coolly and quickly backed off the rubber and calmly threw to catcher Austin Barnes, who grabbed the ball and got his mitt down on Manuel Margot's outstretched hand while the runner's helmet tumbled off and cut his own lip.

Tampa Bay rarely threatened again.

Kershaw's formidable resume has lacked two of the most satisfying achievements: a win deep in the World Series and a championship ring. He has one and lifted himself and his team to the verge of the second.

Mookie Betts and Corey Seager sparked a two-run first inning, and Joc Pederson and Muncy homered off long-ball prone Tyler Glasnow, whose 100 mph heat got burned.

His scraggly dark brown hair dangling with sweat, Kershaw was cruising when Dodgers manager Dave Roberts removed the 32-year-old in favor of right-handed reliever Dustin May after getting two outs on two pitches in the sixth inning.

The mostly pro-Dodgers fans in the pandemic-reduced crowd of 11,437 booed when Roberts walked to the mound, well aware of what happened with the bullpen the previous night, when closer Kenley Jansen wasted a ninth-inning lead in a stunning 8-7 loss.

No matter that some LA players tried to convince Roberts to leave in Kershaw, he was gone.

"Fans, players get caught up in emotion, and I'm emotional, but I still have to have clarity on making decisions," Roberts said. "I can't get caught up in fans' reactions."

Those boos quickly turned to cheers as the Los Angeles rooters saluted Kershaw, a three-time NL Cy Young Award winner, as he walked to the dugout. Kershaw improved to 13-12 in postseason play, including 4-1 this year.

May, Victor Gonzalez and Treinen combined for two-hit scoreless relief. May got five outs, and Gonzalez stranded a pair of runners in the eighth by retiring Randy Arozarena and Brandon Lowe on flyouts.

Treinen got three straight outs after Margot's single leading off the ninth, becoming the fourth Dodgers pitcher with a postseason save.

"Kersh, a lot of credit goes to him for what we've been able to do in this World Series," Treinen said. "There's a tough narrative on him. He's a phenomenal pitcher on the biggest stage."

Kershaw shut down the Rays on two runs and five hits with six strikeouts and two walks. He is 2-0 with a 2.31 ERA in 15 2/3 innings over two starts in this Series with 14 strikeouts and three walks. Kershaw also set a career postseason record with 207 strikeouts, two more than Justin Verlander's previous mark.

Provided a 3-0 lead, Kershaw allowed Tampa Bay to pull within a run in the third when Kiermaier singled, Yandy Díaz tripled on a ball down the right-field line that skipped past Betts and Arozarena singled. The 25-year-old Cuban rookie asked for the ball after his record 27th postseason hit, one more than San Francisco's Pablo Sandoval in 2014.

"I didn't have my stuff like I did in Game 1," Kershaw said. "My slider wasn't there as good as it was, so fortunate to get through there."

Kershaw escaped in the fourth after Margot walked leading off, stole second and continued to third when the ball got away from second baseman Chris Taylor for his second big error in two games. Hunter Renfroe also walked, but Joey Wendle popped out and Willy Adames struck out.

Facing: Starting pitcher Clayton Kershaw got his second victory of the World Series.
KYODO

Joc Pederson hits a home run during the first inning in Game 5.
AP PHOTO/DAVID J. PHILLIP

Manuel Margot is tagged out by Austin Barnes after trying to steal home during the fourth inning in Game 5.

Return to Glory

Mookie Betts scored the go-ahead run and later hit a home run as the Dodgers won their first World Series title since 1988.

October 27, 2020

ARLINGTON, TEXAS — No dogpile, no champagne and a mask on nearly every face — the Los Angeles Dodgers celebrated their first World Series title since 1988 in a manner no one could have imagined prior to the coronavirus pandemic.

They did it without Justin Turner, their red-headed star who received a positive test for COVID-19 in the middle of their clinching victory.

Turner was removed from Los Angeles' 3-1 victory over the Tampa Bay Rays in Game 6 on Tuesday night after registering Major League Baseball's first positive test in 59 days and wasn't on the field as the Dodgers enjoyed the spoils of a title earned during a most unusual season.

"Thanks to everyone reaching out!," Turner said on Twitter. "I feel great, no symptoms at all. Just experienced every emotion you can possibly imagine. Can't believe I couldn't be out there to celebrate with my guys! So proud of this team & unbelievably happy for the City of LA."

Commissioner Rob Manfred confirmed Turner's positive test moments after presenting the World Series trophy to Los Angeles — a jarring reminder of all that's been different in this season where the perennially favored Dodgers finally broke through.

Mookie Betts, who came to the Dodgers to make a World Series difference, had a mad dash to home plate in the sixth inning to put Los Angeles over the top.

The end of a frustrating championship drought for LA — and perhaps just the start for Betts and the Dodgers, whose seventh World Series title was their sixth since leaving Brooklyn to the West Coast in 1958.

Betts bolted from third for the go-ahead run on World Series MVP Corey Seager's infield grounder, then led off the eighth with a punctuating homer.

"I just came to be a part of it. I'm just happy I could contribute," Betts said

Clayton Kershaw was warming in the bullpen when Julio Urias struck out Willy Adames to end it and ran alongside teammates to celebrate in the infield, later joined by family who had been in the bubble with them in North Texas. Players were handed face masks as they gathered, although many of their embraces came mask-free even after Turner's positive test.

The Dodgers had played 5,014 regular season games and were in their 114th postseason game since Orel Hershiser struck out Oakland's Tony Phillips for the final out of the World Series in 1988, the same year Kershaw — the three-time NL Cy Young Award winner who won Games 1 and 5 of this Series — was born in nearby Dallas.

Los Angeles had come up short in the World Series twice in the previous three years. Betts was on the other side two years ago and homered in the clinching Game 5 for the Boston Red Sox, who before this season traded the 2018 AL MVP to the Dodgers. They later gave him a $365 million, 12-year extension that goes until he turns 40 in 2032.

Betts' 3.2-second sprint was just enough to beat the throw by first baseman Ji-Man Choi, pushing Los Angeles ahead 2-1 moments after Rays manager Kevin Cash pulled ace left-hander Blake Snell despite a dominant performance over 5 1/3 innings.

"I'm not exactly sure why," Betts said when asked about the move. "I'm not going to ask any questions. He was pitching a great game."

Randy Arozarena, the powerful Tampa Bay rookie, extended his postseason record with his 10th homer in the first off rookie right-hander Tony Gonsolin, the first of seven Dodgers pitchers. The Rays never got another runner past second base as LA's bullpen gave reliever-reliant Tampa Bay a taste of its own medicine.

About 2 1/2 weeks after the Lakers won the NBA title while finishing their season in the NBA bubble in Orlando, Florida, the Dodgers gave Los Angeles another championship in this year when the novel coronavirus pandemic has delayed, shortened and moved around sports seasons.

Seager, also the NLCS MVP, set Dodgers records with eight homers and 20 RBIs this postseason.

The MLB season didn't start until late July and was abbreviated to 60 games for the shortest regular season since 1878. And the expanded postseason, with 16 teams making it instead of 10, almost went the full distance.

It ended when Urias got the last two out Tampa Bay batters on called third strikes — the 15th and 16 Ks by the Rays, with catcher Austin Barnes stuffing the last pitch in his back pocket. Along with the 11 strikeouts by the Dodgers, it was the most combined strikeouts in a nine-inning World Series game.

Facing: The Dodgers celebrate the final out of Game 6, and their first World Series championship since 1988.
AP PHOTO/DAVID J. PHILLIP

Mookie Betts scores the go-ahead
run past Mike Zunino of Tampa
Bay in the sixth inning of Game 6.
AP PHOTO/DAVID J. PHILLIP

Mookie Betts rounds the bases in front of the Dodgers' dugout after hitting a solo home run to make it 3-1 in the eight inning of Game 6.
AP PHOTO/TONY GUTIERREZ

LOS ANGELES DODGERS

World Series Champions

1955 | 1959 | 1963 | 1965 | 1981 | 1988 | 2020

The Dodgers pose for a photo after their 3-1 win over Tampa Bay in Game 6.
TOM PENNINGTON/GETTY IMAGES